LIFETIME
to
LEGACY

LIFETIME

—— *to* ——

Legacy

A New Vision for Multigenerational Family Businesses

Nike Anani

First published in 2022 by Hambone Publishing
Melbourne, Australia

Editing by Mish Phillips, Jen van Tassel and Emily Stephenson
Cover and interior design by David W. Edelstein

For information about this title, contact:
Nike Anani
na@nikeanani.com
www.nikeanani.com

ISBN 978-1-922357-36-6 (paperback)
ISBN 978-1-922357-37-3 (eBook)

Contents

Introduction

his is not a book on technical elements of a family enterprise, like strategic business planning, operations, estate planning, and wealth planning. Those are important elements but not sufficient to guarantee the future success of your enterprise. Rather, it is a book on relational elements, i.e. how to build greater connectivity in your family to aid in moving your family enterprise from lifetime to legacy. Said another way, it is not about protecting the future of your family enterprise, but about creating the family enterprise of the future. That, I believe, is the way to move your family enterprise from lifetime to legacy.

Legacy is distinct from sustainability. Sustainability refers to maintaining the status quo to just survive, whereas legacy goes beyond that to incorporate not just maintaining but also creating, in order to thrive. Sustainability refers to transitioning, whereas legacy refers to transforming.

Key to moving from lifetime to legacy is creating future-focused enterprises. This entails enabling innovation and creativity such that you are able to create new opportunities that would be viable in the future through regeneration, renewal, and reinvention. This book focuses on how to manage family relationships to unlock that very innovation and creativity, to maximize the intellectual diversity needed to bring about transformation.

Family business owners are busy! I know all too well. So I wrote a book that I would be inspired to read: it is practical, it is entertaining, and it is to the point. For the past decade, I have devoted my career to the world of family business, both as an insider and as a consultant. Most of these lessons are from my practical experience leading our family enterprise in Nigeria, as well as from consulting with clients, delivering training workshops, and speaking in front of family business audiences.

You will find a simple framework that will change the way you see your family, your business, and yourself, focusing on the relational and psychological elements of family business.

If you are seeking a simple, hands-on guide with lots of tips on building a legacy enterprise, you will appreciate this book. If you are seeking practical, non-academic lessons to use right away to navigate generational transition, you will find it easy to use.

Inside This Book

In this book I clarify, simplify, and demystify the world that is family business, particularly from an African perspective. There is a lot to learn, and these learnings are simple, practical, and implementable such that you can use them right away.

Among the lessons covered:

- ᔌ Common mistakes family business owners make and how to overcome them
- ᔌ The nuances of family businesses and why a generational transition is not automatic
- ᔌ Why only 2% of businesses in Africa have failed to move past generation one and how we can address that
- ᔌ Why it's so hard for business founders to let go, and how to support them on their exit journey
- ᔌ Why next gens grapple with championing change in their family enterprises and how to support them
- ᔌ Why it's so hard to talk about money, death, and emotions in business families and how to break the ice
- ᔌ Why connected families are important, and the case for individual family members to stay together, rather than go their separate ways
- ᔌ How you can go on to develop connectivity in your family across generations and within generations

You'll find stories of family businesses from my journey advising business families and as co-founder of African Family Firms—the largest pan-African community of family business owners; identities of the individuals and companies have been disguised. By the end of the book, you'll be equipped with the mindset and roadmap required to ensure that your family is able to think more collaboratively and creatively, so that your family enterprise can move from lifetime to legacy.

To get the most out of this book, I recommend reading it as

a family. I also recommend not just consuming the content like a Netflix binge, but also seeking to do the exercises.

About Me

I was born into a business family; however, I went my own way for many years. After a career in Corporate Tax International at Deloitte UK, I was immersed first-hand as a second-generation family business leader and owner in our enterprise. I soon became obsessed with legacy enterprises and then dedicated my career to the field.

Ever since I was a young girl I've been fascinated by human behavior—analysing, dissecting, and watching. It's a surprise that I didn't study psychology at university, but economics. I was often coined a psychic by my friends as I could predict and project how people would behave in different scenarios.

The more I studied and served family businesses, the more I realized the world of human behavior and legacy enterprises were intrinsically linked. The fascination with human behavior took on new heights as it became clear that for our family enterprises to stand the test of time, they would have to transform, and the key to transforming was ensuring that families are able to think collaboratively and creatively. The heart of it was relational, not just technical.

Nurturing this relational element has tangible quantitative benefits. For one, it yields engagement: Gallup studies show that where there is strong connection with one's work and colleagues, businesses enjoy higher productivity, better quality products, and increased profitability. Secondly, it yields trust: according to Harvard Business Review,[1] people at high-trust companies report 50% higher productivity and 76% more engagement than those at low-trust companies.

This book seeks to teach family owners how to be better connected to unlock collaborative creativity. I believe that families seeking to build future-focused enterprises must optimize their relationships to draw upon the intellectual diversity they are gifted with. Families have the answers within them; what they need is some guidance to unlock their potential. This book serves to do just that, and also to be fun, relatable, and entertaining.

Enjoy!

CHAPTER 1

Creating a Transformational Business

Multigenerational success requires transformation, not transition. Transitioning refers to "the process of changing from one state or condition to another," whereas transforming refers to "a marked change in form, nature, or appearance." Family enterprises often face negative extraneous setbacks like economic recessions, political volatility, regulatory changes, technological changes, or global pandemics that become drivers of change. Rather than just responding to these setbacks, families need to transform their enterprises by setting up new product/service lines, expanding into new geographies, setting up new businesses, making new investments, and/or pursuing joint ventures.

By being proactive in driving change rather than reactive in being malleable in the face of outside change, family enterprises become future-proofed for upcoming generations. As they transform, they become transformational.

Future-proofing the Enterprise

Can we debunk something real quick? When we say we want to build a future-proofed enterprise, we do not mean that we want to guarantee the success and/or existence of your businesses and investments. Instead, what we mean is that even in the face of setbacks, your family is able to create something new. Future-proofing looks more broadly at how we can continue the family legacy of entrepreneurship through regeneration, renewal, and reinvention to ensure that the enterprise is relevant in the future. It's not about guaranteeing the future of the business, but about creating the business of the future.

Many families are active in a diverse range of business activities, so it is possible that a given business may fail, but the overall enterprise flourishes. Future-proofing is not an insurance against entrepreneurial failure (i.e. a given operating business going bankrupt or ceasing to exist). In fact, I would argue that entrepreneurial failure is often a currency for future success of the family, as through collective wisdom, knowledge, and intelligence, the family is able to reflect on its history, learn from it, and forge a stronger future. Future-proofing, on the other hand, is about know-how. Future-proofing requires passing down and building upon an entrepreneurial legacy.

Legacy is defined as something that's transmitted by or received from an ancestor or predecessor from the past. Peter Strople once said, "Legacy is not leaving something for people. It's leaving something in people." Likewise, the concept of an entrepreneurial legacy is not the passing down of businesses and assets for descendants, but rather leaving them with the ability to create and maintain business and assets themselves. It is where family members are able to recreate financial and social value across generations, drawing on the family's collective well of triumphs and trials in its past, such that they can rebuild in their present, accumulating resilience for the future.

The continued entrepreneurial legacy has great implications not just for enterprise activities but also for social value creation. The entrepreneurial mindset of identifying a problem and creating a solution that provides compelling value for stakeholders can equally be extended to social issues, and often business families do so through philanthropy and impact investing. Thus, this legacy allows for the preservation of the entrepreneurial mindset over generations, which has a significant ripple effect. The passing of an entrepreneurial legacy is about skill: it's not the passing of a what, but the passing of a how.

Why Are Transformational Family Enterprises Important?

It is critical that your family enterprise is future-proofed because not only does your family gain, but also the business, your local community, your nation, and the world gains, for the following reasons.

Protection from the plague of poverty

Growing up in Nigeria surrounded by high levels of absolute and relative poverty left a mark on me. I would see many destitute people without access to food, education, shelter, or healthcare. Unfortunately, this poverty worsened over time;

we currently have 87 million people living in severe poverty in Nigeria, which is approximately half of our population. We've been coined the "poverty capital" of the world. It's nothing to be proud of. And we have one of the highest youth unemployment rates globally. It seems that we are on a slippery slope rushing into deeper poverty.

This poverty has devastating impacts beyond the pocket—it also affects the mind. French philosopher Michel de Montaigne said, "Poverty of goods is easily cured; poverty of the mind is irreparable." Poverty of goods can be cured with the presence of money, whereas poverty of the mind has long-lasting, significant effects.

In Some Consequences of Having Too Little, authors Shah, Mullainathan and Shafir explain that "Scarcity changes how people allocate attention: it leads them to engage more deeply in some problems, while neglecting others." They find that low-income individuals often play lotteries, fail to enrol in assistance programs, save too little, and borrow too much.

This indicates that scarcity can lead to people making sub-optimal decisions through altering of how their attention is allocated. For instance, it can force one to be short-termist. In addition it can force one to be focused on consuming rather than investing, and it can force one to tend to prioritize immediate cash flow over longer-term returns on investment. As a result, it can act as friction, stopping one from embracing a legacy entrepreneurial mindset and instead focusing on a lifetime mindset.

Poverty also robs time. In their book, Scarcity, authors Sendhil Mullainathan and Eldar Shafir show that scarcity affects the way people manage their time. Those less financially wealthy are often time-poor. So much time is spent hustling trying to find the next source of cash flow to meet their basic needs that they have inadequate time to focus on changing their situation for the better. Yet time, not money, is arguably the most important asset we all have, as it is the only non-renewable resource. Valuing time over money is key to creating true financial freedom.

Poverty tends to compound over generations. Families struggle to break free from the shackles of generational poverty. It need not be this way, as generational enterprise is the antidote to generational poverty. John F. Kennedy said, "A rising tide lifts all boats"—the development of generational enterprise not only lifts the family out of poverty, but also lifts surrounding communities through the creation of wealth.

Lastly, poverty is undignified. Jacqueline Novogratz said, "The opposite of poverty is dignity. It is having a choice, having opportunity, having agency over who you are in your life and what you are capable of doing." We all deserve dignity.

To leave a legacy

Legacy is defined as something transmitted by or received from an ancestor or predecessor from the past, which includes tangible and intangible objects. It also includes narratives both over time and space. Legacies can be contemporaneous, i.e. it is possible to craft a living legacy; to not just leave a legacy but to also live one's legacy.

In addition, our family businesses are a great vehicle to pass down our legacies over time. We can pass down our family values from generation to generation, transmitting our culture and heritage. It is important that we are conscious about becoming legacy architects.

To craft our narrative and export our stories

As Africans, it is especially important that we carefully craft our living legacies, because the world needs to understand who we are right now. Too often there is only one story shared about our continent. Certain narratives were upheld to maintain power over the African continent, stemming from the era of colonialism. These narratives were then passed down from generation to generation. However, the message that we have received has been distorted: the truth of who we were and who we are differs greatly from the image and the narrative that has been portrayed, both by ourselves and by outsiders. It is therefore important that we craft our own narratives.

I remember watching Chimamanda Adichie's The Danger of the Single Story speech on TED Talks in my dormitory room in my first year of university, and for the first time I felt permission to embody the fullness of who I was. To not feel limited to a narrow definition of what it meant to be an African.

Chimamanda's message not only liberated me, but it also impressed upon me the importance of sharing diverse stories about the continent.

I was having a conversation with Zita Nikoletta Verbenyi on my podcast, *The Connected Generation*, and she stressed the importance of sharing stories, and the importance of controlling narratives contextually. She mentioned that not only is this critical for us as individuals and families, but also as societies. Whoever has control over the narrative does the framing, though often what is left outside of the frame is information critical to understanding the full story.

It is like in photography: a photograph is a representation

of a point in time and space. The photographer chooses which aspect of reality to represent by deciding on what to capture within the frame and what to leave outside of the frame. What is left out of the picture can be an essential part of the photography, telling a different story, and the audience may see an image that is not a fair representation of the reality.

As Africans, we have to be conscious to become our own photographers, deciding what is inside the frame and what is outside the frame to showcase stories that are representative and authentic. Affinity and representation matter. They give people permission to be themselves as they see possibility modeled out before them by a person who is similar to them. We have an opportunity to tell diverse stories of who we are, through the export of our ideas, culture, entertainment, goods, and services among ourselves and to the global stage.

The single story of Africa is dangerous, as we are a continent with such rich heterogeneity. With a population of 1.2 billion people and over 3,000 tribes, we need to showcase multiple stories highlighting our rich diversity. Our family businesses can become vehicles to export our stories to the global stage.

To be a social solution and a global change

The reality of our world is that wealth opens doors, because often financial capital and social capital go hand in hand. Wealth-owners have become affluent, not only because of their access to financial resources, but also because of their networks and reputations. In addition, as wealth owners become affluent, they have access to more networks and enhanced reputation.

The relationship between financial capital and social capital is one both of causation and correlation.

As one ascends the financial ladder, typically one also ascends the social ladder, gaining access to more information, resources, and entrepreneurship and investment opportunities. In addition, this social capital typically expands geographically: one enjoys access to a network of global decision-makers who have significant influence on our world.

The risk we face is that Africans may be left out of such networks, and thus lack the opportunity to contribute to critical global conversations on political, social, and environmental change—the conversations that are driving the future of our world. We need access to such rooms. By 2050, Africa is estimated to double her population, at which point one in four people on the globe will be African. Our voices desperately need to be heard, as we are one of the greatest beneficiaries of such decisions.

The multigenerational success of African family enterprises gives us opportunities to make an impact on a global scale. It allows for the next generation to utilize their financial, social, intellectual, and political capital to create social change. It is projected that over the next 50 years the world will see the largest wealth transfer in history, with inheritors set to receive between $30–70 trillion. Africa is home to 15% of the world's total population, yet only 0.9% of the world's high net worth individuals.[2] If we anticipate a doubling of our population over the next 30 years, this relative proportion of global wealth is likely to fall.

Therefore, our children and grandchildren may not be enabled to be changemakers and solutionaries in our world, which is sad because we face a greater extent of social issues than any other continent: out of the 20 countries in the world with the worst food and nutrition security, 19 are in Africa, more than two in five African adults cannot read or write, and there's a pending food insecurity crisis. Not to be a harbinger of doom or anything, but just to highlight that unless something drastically changes, the needle is unlikely to shift.

So, we need more Africans engaging in shaping change through global forums like World Economic Forum, to rub shoulders with business, political, and academic leaders and shape the continent's future. In addition, we need more Africans represented at bodies like NEXUS, where they connect with other philanthropists, impact investors, meet social entrepreneurs, and build collaborations. These collaborations with global counterparts are key, as the scale of the issues our world faces requires cross-cultural collaborations to solve.

I believe that business families occupy a unique position in society to drive such social change. Unlike other institutions, they tend to be longtermist in their orientation, and they tend to be communal, thinking about other stakeholders beyond shareholders. However, there's scope to optimize this beyond the lifetime of the founder. To see their continued impact over generations, it is key that family enterprises are future-proofed through transforming, not just transitioning.

CHAPTER 2

Obstacles to Building a Transformational Business

About ten years ago, I had a strange debilitating nerve pain in my hands, shoulders, and neck that was exacerbated by writing. Even sending a text message left me in agony. Over a period of two weeks, this pain spread to my arms, back, and legs.

I visited several GPs and specialist doctors, and all were completely baffled, as all the investigations—blood tests, MRI scans, X-rays, etc.—indicated that I was perfectly healthy. By this point I was unable to work, and I felt depressed and confused about my future.

I didn't learn the cause until I visited a rheumatologist four months later, who realized I was hyper flexible and had a weak core. This combination, she hypothesized, was causing these strange symptoms. Finally, I had a cause, which was a huge relief, as I was starting to question my own sanity, asking myself whether the pain was a figment of my imagination. The previous doctors had been treating the presenting symptoms, i.e. the muscular pain and nerve pain, but had not identified the root cause. It was only the rheumatologist who was able to do so, providing hope for a sustainable recovery.

Similarly, it's important when seeking to future-proof your family enterprise that you do not just focus on the presenting symptoms, i.e. the visible metrics of the enterprise such as revenues, profits, cash flow, staff productivity, extent of diversification, returns on investment, etc. When unaware of the root cause, there's a temptation to make assumptions about what an appropriate solution would be, like my previous doctors had done. However, "Assuming is the root of all disappointments," as Rogienel Reyes said, and it is unlikely to yield an effective solution. Therefore, we must perform a root cause analysis to identify effective solutions.

Root cause analysis is a method used in science and engineering to identify root causes of faults in order to problem solve. The goals of root cause analysis are to:

1) Uncover the root cause of an issue;
2) Understand how to rectify the issue; and
3) Apply the learnings from the analysis to prevent future issues.

While it is important to treat symptoms for short-term relief, this is insufficient. The problem solver needs to focus not only on the correction and treatment of symptoms but also on the root causes. Therefore, to be able to carve out an effective solution for future-proofing family enterprises, we must conduct a root analysis of either why families have failed to do so in the past, or of why they have succeeded in doing so.

Common Mistakes

Many business owners struggle to build transformational enterprises due to common mistakes and myths they tend to hold. These include:

Working in the business, not ON the business

I remember the first time I heard Amy Porterfield, online marketing guru, explain to entrepreneurs the distinction between working in your business and working on your business. She said that many business owners are too deep in the details of day-to-day operations, so that they lack time to work on strategic initiatives on the business to grow it. Entrepreneurs need to ensure they don't fall into the trap where they work so hard IN the business that they do not have the time and mental capacity to work ON it. Working in the business involves administration, meeting clients, and answering queries, whereas working on the business involves strategic planning, learning and education, goal setting, automating processes, and capacity building.

It was an "aha" moment, as I realized that a similar phenomenon exists with business families.

Many of us are often so focused on working in our enterprises that we neglect working on our enterprises. Such people are conscious operators rather than conscious owners. To successfully transition your enterprise across generations, you need to think more strategically, moving from knowing the minute details of operations to having a broader overview of the enterprise.

One of my favorite proverbs is an Igbo one that says, "Whenever one wakes up is his own morning." You need to have a similar awakening to move your enterprise successfully into the future. It is morning now and your priorities have changed. Both the family and the enterprise are facing greater levels of complexity. In light of this complexity, it's clear to see that continuing as an operator is detrimental to the future of the enterprise.

To successfully transition, you need to focus more on your ownership role, and on strategic decision-making rather than operational matters. This entails becoming adept at driving the investments, people, governance, and culture of the family enterprise.

In addition, there needs to be an awakening to the full scope of your ownership role and the totality of the resources you have at your disposal. These resources are not just financial, but also social, intellectual, and spiritual. They're not only sourced from the founder, but from the entire family. As a conscious owner, you need to build connectivity in the family.

In a family enterprise setting, working on the enterprise largely involves working on the family. The family is the skeleton of the enterprise. Without it, the enterprise lacks framework, support, movement, and regulation. It is the most important component and yet, it is often paid the least attention. Research suggests that a more collective family orientation is needed in the second generation (G2) to succeed.[3] This necessitates focus on family connectivity.

It's technical NOT relational

A few years ago, I was at a networking event. A gentleman asked me the dreaded what do you do? question. I found it difficult to explain what I did in a concise manner that would get the message across. Often, people would ask several clarifying questions to really understand my work. I explained, "I help families build legacy enterprises, by building stronger relationships between the generations in the family." He said, "But how does that help in building multigenerational enterprises? Isn't that what trustees are for?"

I went on to explain that trusts are just a piece in the puzzle. The solution requires not only the technical but also the relational. Legal structuring, estate planning, and legal documentation are important, but without addressing the family relationships these plans will fail to come to life. They will remain lifeless documents that sit on the family bookshelf, gathering dust. To see them come to life, the family dynamics must also be addressed. Thus, succession planning must address both the technical and the relational.

This is because the technical is built on a foundation of the relational. Therefore the relational must come first. In addition, the technical assumes linearity, whereas family, by its very nature, is non-linear. It is a unit full of emotion. The technical requires the family to implement, though they may struggle to have clarity of oneness, to communicate and collaborate. So relational dynamics and conflict can create a roadblock and can lead to irrational decision-making.

For instance, a common scenario is a founder of a business setting up a trust for his/her family members. The trust is to own the family business and family assets. The founder believes that this trust would provide financial security for the family. The founder has decided that all the surviving family members are to be decision-makers. He/she set up this trust without conversations with their spouse and children aligning on the purpose of the enterprise, values, vision, and mission: they pursued the technical without the relational.

Upon their death, the children find out about the trust for the first time. They are struggling to collaborate in making joint decisions; they constantly squabble and fail to have consensus. The family wealth becomes a source of friction rather than a source of power. Due to incessant fighting, the children decide to go their separate ways and divide the estate. This also damages their family relationship.

The truth is that we are emotional beings who occasionally think, rather than thinking beings who occasionally emote. What is "rational" may not hold in our families. To ensure that we successfully plan for the future, it is key to not only invest on the technical but also invest on the relational.

It's a revolution NOT an evolution

Marie Antoinette, former Queen of France, was said to have replied, "Let them eat cake!" when told that her subjects had no bread. Her insensitive, callous remark is said to have triggered the French Revolution in 1787. The revolution completely changed the relationship between the rulers and the subjects and redefined the nature of political power in France.

Revolutions lead to sudden and dramatic changes. These can occur not only in political spheres but also in family enterprises. Evolutions and revolutions both refer to change. However, evolution is a slow and gradual change, while revolution is a sudden, dramatic, and complete change. It's important to note that the speed of change does not necessarily determine the size of impact. Arguably, evolutions lead to greater positive impact, as the risk of failure is significantly lower than that of revolutions.

In a family enterprise, a common revolution is when the founder passes away and the siblings are now in the power seat. Often, siblings will exercise their powers by changing everything suddenly—changing the advisors, changing the strategy, changing key people, and restructuring. According to a PWC Global Private Banking/Wealth Management Survey in 2011, only 2% of heirs will retain their parents' advisors.

A common difficulty they face in pursuing a revolution is that often they have very little experience working together and so have not formed the cadence of an effective, productive partnership. They pursue drastic change while their team is at an infancy stage of development. This is quite risky and often disrupts not only the enterprise but also the family.

Instead, business families should pursue evolutions. Rather than a drastic transfer of power from the first to the second generation, this can be more gradual, whereby siblings enjoy gradually increased power, authority, and influence over the family enterprise during the life of the founder. In addition, they become intentional about becoming sibling partners, because partnership takes time, practice, and intentionality.

To see this evolution of increasing involvement and prominence of the rising generation, there must be the right enabling environment: an environment that is open to new ideas. An evolution of inclusivity.

It's about individual rulership NOT collective leadership

Our first-generation family enterprises are often character-ized by a dominant founder who makes unilateral decisions. They are typically surrounded by helpers, who implement the vision of the founder. While this founder-centricity gives an advantage, as the enterprise is able to make quick decisions, this centricity unfortunately can become detrimental as we navigate a generational change. It is key that instead we develop a culture of collaboration.

Through a culture of collaboration, we can move from being governed by an individual ruler to being governed by collective leaders. Rulers exercise ultimate power and authority over their people. Leaders, on the other hand, guide and direct. Rulers impose; leaders influence. Rulers have subjects; leaders have willing followers. As we say in Africa, "Just because the lizard nods his head doesn't mean he's in agreement." A ruler is often surrounded by subjects that nod, but don't necessarily agree.

In the past, our families have chosen rulers who would suc-ceed the founder. They have traditionally tapped the eldest son to take over the enterprise and to exercise ultimate power and authority over all other family members. But we know that this strategy has not been very successful, leading to many a court battle and many a divided family.

There's an alternative: instead of choosing a dominant ruler who is surrounded by helpers, we can have collective leadership among the siblings. Here, siblings see themselves as co-builders of the enterprise, and they share and discover ideas and co-create solutions together. They do not just nod in compli-ance, but they agree.

Here, all rising generation members are leaders, whether or not they work in the business or family office, whether or not they are on the pitch or on the sidelines. Whoever is then elected as the CEO of the business, family office or family council is seen as a representative of the collective. This way, the question of who will succeed the founder is not as fractious, as all family members are assured that their ideas, thoughts, and perspectives will influence decision-making, rather than be imposed.

Many families seek to pass on the baton from generation to generation, but few will succeed in doing so. These families navigate increased complexity as they seek to transition beyond generation one. Legacy building is likened to construction in that it takes time; specifically, it takes time to pass on the entrepreneurial mindset to the next generation. Like construction, legacy building requires a plan; no one builds a building without architectural drawings. Similarly, legacies are not built by happenstance, but require careful planning. Lastly, like construction, legacy building involves a collaborative effort to see that it is executed according to plan: the family has to come together and collectively work together to co-create the enterprise of the future.

CHAPTER 3

The Importance of Connection

The journey to multigenerational success requires transformation. That's achieved by addressing both the relational and the technical, infusing the emotional with the intellectual. It requires a gradual evolution of power, authority, and influence of the rising generation during the lifetime of the founder, as opposed to a drastic revolution upon his/her death. Lastly, it requires going on a journey from individual rulership to collective leadership of the family enterprise. In summary, it requires your family to be connected.

Why Connection Matters

Professor Dennis Jaffe, a leading family business consultant and researcher, conducted a global study in 2018, Resilience of 100-Year Enterprises, which evaluated enduring family businesses that had lasted over 100 years. It evaluated 100 families across 20 countries and described their journeys over more than six generations.

Jaffe found these families to be, "More than businesses; they also share a family culture of relationships, values, traditions, respect, and learning that underlies their business capabilities. Their family culture is the foundation of their business acumen."[4] He described them as "Generative families." Not only did Jaffe allude to the family being a bedrock of the enterprise, but he also explained that these generative families were resilient across generations due to an awareness of the range of resources they had available, but also due to their coming together to use these resources to sustain and create something new in the enterprise.

They had focused on cultivating the family through investing in education and development, through family events, through cultivating the extended family, and nurturing the family values. These families in effect were well connected. Successful family enterprises, like members of a soccer team, have a greater chance of winning when well connected.

The ability of the enterprise to reinvent itself through geographic expansion, product expansion, new investments, and/or new joint ventures, for instance, depended on the family's ability to come together. The connectivity of the generations allowed for each generation to contribute something new to the enterprise, and this newness kept the enterprises future-focused. This connectivity, though unobservable, was critical in allowing for a resilient enterprise to emerge.

What Connection Means

Business families often face setbacks that necessitate change. We need to be able to transform our enterprises to be future-proofed despite these negative conditions. Key to transforming is connecting. The irony is that while we are in the fourth industrial revolution where we are experiencing a rise in artificial intelligence and digital transformations of our societies, enterprise transformations will still be human-led.

Connection enables diversity of thought, and co-creation of solutions. It triggers collaborative intelligence. In a world of increasing complexity, what we need to thrive as business owners is to become adept at decision-making. Those who enjoy greater quality and quantity of ideas have unrivaled advantage; however, that only comes about when we are truly connected, not divided or affiliated.

Connected means we are united, not uniform: we celebrate differences in one another, appreciating that our differences in age, gender, tribe, race, and experience contribute to our unique insights and perspectives. The more diversity we have as individuals, the stronger the group is. Incidentally, our families are endowed with natural diversity in age and gender that other institutions do not necessarily enjoy. We can maximize this endowment by facilitating collective co-creation of ideas. This will give an excellent advantage, as in this increasingly fast-paced business world, the ability to make quick decisions is key to flourishing.

Connected families have independence as well as interdependence: we prioritize the good of the collective family as well as the individual. They are connected both vertically and horizontally, enjoying age and gender inclusion. They are united but not uniform; they have clarity of oneness. Such families provide a range of support (emotional, esteem, network, informational, and financial) to family members and draw on support from a range of family members at times of need. Families who nurture these connections effectively create the very breeding ground for transformation.

A family enterprise is like a car, while the family members are like the gears. The car is able to travel faster the better connected the gears are. The connection is a necessary enabler to ensure the car moves with speed. Interdependence is an enabler to ensure the family enterprise successfully moves toward the future.

Aristotle said, "The whole is greater than the sum of its parts." Through greater levels of interdependence, your family can enjoy better results than if individual family members were to go separate ways.

How Connection Works

By investing in clarity of oneness, communicating, and collaborating, your family can move from being affiliated to being connected. As a result, you'll move:

- From having transactional conversations to having transformational conversations. In these conversations, you see possibilities in yourself as an individual, as a family, and as a family enterprise. You enjoy cohesion and trust as you pursue possibility.

⚘ From lone genius to collaborative intelligence. You work and think together. You see your differences as a strength as you cultivate intellectual diversity. You move from an ask-and-tell model with regards to collation of ideas, to a share-and-discover model. As a result, you all co-create solutions, as opposed to co-exist. Through collaborative intelligence, you are better able to solve enterprise challenges due to setbacks, increasing productivity, creativity, and innovation.

⚘ From lifetime to legacy. Through discovery of ideas, you are able to adapt and transform your enterprise to be relevant, becoming future-proofed. Through future-proofing and continued longevity, your enterprise continues to generate employment, be a helm in communities, and precipitate social change. In so doing, you enjoy a legacy of transformation and leave a transformational legacy.

Vertical Versus Horizontal Connections

One common mistake family enterprises make when engaging in succession planning is focusing on vertical connections and neglecting horizontal ones. Vertical connections (connecting above) refer to connections across different generations, i.e. between generation one and generation two, whereas horizontal connections (connecting across) refer to connections within the same generation. To successfully transition their enterprises, families must both connect above and connect across.

This is because as the enterprise crosses the generational line, the baton of decision-making will be passed from the founder to the siblings. The siblings must already be a cohesive team, so that they can hit the ground running. The challenge is that team formation takes time, practice, and preparation. Siblings don't emerge as collective leaders, they practice it. They don't emerge as collective visionaries, they prepare for it. Families should not wait until the inevitable to start the process; they should start this preparation of connecting across during the lifetime of the founder.

A similar phenomenon plays out in sports teams: successful teams also have both strong vertical and horizontal connections. Vertical connections refer to connections with other team players in different positions. In soccer, a goalkeeper must maintain good connections with defenders, midfielders, and forwards. On the other hand, horizontal connections refer to connections with other team players in the same category of positions: a center-back defender must maintain good connections with a sweeper defender and a full-back defender.

Similarly, successful family enterprises must maintain strong vertical and horizontal family connections. They must be connected across and above, enjoying both intragenerational connections and intergenerational connections, drawing on resources of all family members.

Why Start Now?

In his book, Atomic Habits, James Clear explains the concept of the Margin of Safety. Margin of Safety is a principle encouraging one to be proactive in protecting oneself from unforeseen problems and challenges by building a buffer. He says:

> *Maintain a margin of safety—even when it's going well. Rich people go bankrupt chasing even more wealth. Fit people get injured chasing personal records. Productive people become ineffective taking on too many projects. Don't let your ambition ruin your position."*

Similarly, we also need to maintain a margin of safety as we build our enterprises, seeking to be intentional about connecting before we have to, by connecting as a family during the lifetime of the founder.

This is because connecting takes time: we are not just connecting at the head, but we are also connecting at the heart. Matters of the heart come to the fore over time as we gradually build trust to share with one another. Connecting also takes intentionality; it only happens in conducive environments, and it cannot be done on the fly, in a rush, or as an afterthought. It requires investing time and energy to connect. Connecting takes practice: moving from a founder-led enterprise to a siblings-led enterprise requires a lot of change. Change is not easy and comes with deliberate practice.

It is important that we invest in connecting even before we have to, so that we become "Stronger than we need to be, leaving room for the unexpected."[5]

CHAPTER 4

The Circle of Safety

esearch suggests that connection leads to increased engagement; a sense of belonging, camaraderie, and kinship fosters trust and loyalty. Individuals who are better connected are more likely to contribute, expend energy, be better committed, and take ownership in groups. Simon Sinek describes this as a Circle of Safety where there is a "Feeling of belonging, shared values and a deep sense of empathy which dramatically enhances trust, cooperation and problem solving."[6]

The Circle of Safety for intragenerational and intergenerational connections in families generates an environment that is conducive to greater problem solving. This is particularly important in the hour we find ourselves in, where family enterprises are facing a 21st century volatile, uncertain, complex, and ambiguous (VUCA) world that is fast-changing and disrupting industries and business models.

Connection and Building Resilience

Over the next century, the world will see even greater technological changes in artificial intelligence, blockchain, big data, and robotics that will rapidly transform the economic and business landscapes. Therefore, more than ever, family enterprises must be capable of problem solving by building agile, adaptable, future-focused organizations, otherwise they will fail to ensure the continued success of their enterprises.

Greater connectivity within the family creates an enabling environment for the rising generation to contribute their ideas to the family enterprise through geographic expansion, new product/services, joint ventures, and/or investments. These can take form as entrepreneurial or intrapreneurial ventures. These new activities are critical in making the business family more resilient: through the contribution of new activities, the family enterprise becomes increasingly diversified in asset type, currency, geography, and industry. As a result, the enterprise is better able to withstand disruptive business environments and thus be future-proofed.

In addition to the disruptive landscape, family enterprises find themselves in a world that is laden with social challenges. The effective connectivity of the generations will maximize their impact and speed up their transition to more conscious capitalism. Increasingly, investors are expected to use their wealth to affect social change; the rising generation in particular has a longing to be change makers who not only maximize financial returns but also maximize social change through non-traditional capitalist business models, such as ESG investing, impact investing, social entrepreneurship, and philanthropy.

Connection and Family Roles

In addition, these connections enable the family to be flexible with regards to the roles family members can play in the enterprise. As the enterprise evolves beyond generation one, responsibilities in the enterprise move away from being concentrated on an individual to being shared among the collective. In addition, the responsibilities move away from being concentrated on operatorship to strategy.

As a result, there is an increasing number of functions required to sustain the enterprise as it becomes more formalized and intentional, including executive management of the operating businesses, board of directors of the operating businesses, chair of the family council, executive management of the family office, board of directors of the family office, executive management of the family foundation, and board of trustees of the foundation. Incidentally, rising generation members are less interested in leadership of the family business in the battlefield and would rather get involved from the sidelines. Connected families are better able to identify different strengths and aspirations of individual family members, and can therefore have them contribute appropriately and collaboratively.

Qualitative Connections

It is important to note that effective connection is not only transactional but it is also relational. Transactional connection refers to the ability to "connect" on the enterprise alone, where the family is able to communicate, collaborate, and have clarity on business alone. With transactional connections, families are able to jointly analyze technical issues and make collective decisions to yield positive performance.

Relational connection, on the other hand, goes beyond the technical and looks to nurturing the personal relationships in the family. It looks to developing deeper, more permanent, high-quality relationships with family members. Connection is not just about the head, but it is also about the heart. It is not just about the quantitative, it is also about the qualitative.

Decision-making is at the center of business families. However, most wrongly assume that effective decision-making is rational, based on quantitative analysis and using critical thinking alone. In reality, it is from the heart that we make decisions, not from the head. As is often said, "We are not cognitive beings that on occasion feel, but we are emotional beings that on occasion think."

Effective decision-making fuses both left and right brain, including also qualitative data, behavioral insights, and emotions. This results in a richer and fuller decision-making process.

In his book, The Future of Management, Gary Hamel writes:

> Sit in on a typical management meeting—to discuss strategy, budgets, employees, or anything else—and not only will you observe a distinct lack of right-brain thinking, you'll also hear virtually nothing that suggests the participants have hearts. Beauty. Truth. Love. Service. Wisdom. Justice. Freedom. Compassion. These are the moral imperatives that have aroused human beings to extraordinary accomplishments down through the ages."

For families to make better decisions, they need to include right-brain thinking. They need to engage not only their heads but also their hearts. It is the skills connected to the heart that give rise to extraordinary accomplishments.

Brené Brown defines connection as, "The energy that exists between people when they feel seen, heard and valued; when they can give and receive without judgment; and when they derive sustenance and strength from the relationship." I believe she is referring to a relational connection in her definition. Therefore, to connect at the heart, family members need to see, hear, and value each other. It is only when these members feel seen, heard, and valued that they will then see others, hear others, and contribute value themselves.

The Importance of Heart

Engaging the heart gives rise to conscious families. Conscious families elevate the importance of humanity in their enterprise. Rather than being enterprise-centric, where the focus is on profit and returns maximization, they are human-centric, seeking to add value to the lives of their customers, employees, and communities, and how to maximize that value. Financial returns are a by-product of said value. Conscious families are just as driven by the quantitative as well as the qualitative: community, reputation, harmony, and relationships are often as important as profit, productivity, and performance.

Families that are connected at the heart are able to make better decisions in a disrupted world.

The world is in unprecedented times, and as a result it is increasingly difficult to measure risk, describe probabilities, and quantify opportunities with certainty. The use of qualitative decision-making therefore enables families to operate in this new paradigm.

Families that are connected at the heart are richer, as they experience greater levels of satisfaction and happiness. However, business families are often disconnected at the heart, with very lonely individuals who hide their hearts from each other. For example, founders are often plagued with anxiety, fear, and the emotional burden of leadership, whereas next gens are wrestling complex identities toward wealth and stewardship anxiety. Family members have to bridge this gap and nurture their relational connection.

Family members connecting at the heart increase the family capital.

This is due to the Law of Reciprocity, which states that when someone does a favor for you, you have a need to do something nice in return.

In Influence, the classic book on the science of persuasion, psychologist Robert Cialdini cites one study demonstrating the law of reciprocity in action: restaurant servers who gave diners a free mint at the end of their meal saw their tips increase by 3%. Those who gave two mints and mentioned to the diners that they were only supposed to give one experienced a 14% tip increase.

Connecting at the heart leads to belonging.

Brené Brown defines belonging as:

> ...The spiritual practice of believing in and belonging to yourself so deeply that you can share your most authentic self with the world and find sacredness in both being a part of something and standing alone in the wilderness. True belonging does not require you to change who you are; it requires you to be who you are."

Family members need to feel safe to project their authentic selves with one another. They need to not only belong to their individual selves, but they also need to belong to each other.

Brown also explains that belonging is distinct from fitting in; she often says, "The opposite of belonging is fitting in." Fitting in is when we blend in like chameleons, rather than having the courage to stand alone like leopards. Chameleons have the ability to change color to blend in to their habitats to protect themselves from intruders: it's a defense mechanism.

Leopards on the other hand are solitary, stealthy predators. They are not afraid of living life alone and are able to kill prey up to three times their weight—they are attackers. Family members need the courage to stand alone like leopards, knowing that they will belong to themselves and belong to each other. To do so, the family needs to have a culture of inclusion.

The Business Case for Inclusion

Research suggests that organizations that are inclusive are two times more likely to meet or exceed their financial targets, three times as likely to be high-performing, six times more likely to be innovative and agile, and eight times more likely to achieve better business outcomes than those that are not.[7] This is because inclusive teams allow for diversity of thought.

Not only do inclusive teams lead to stronger collective performance, but they also lead to greater affirmation of the individuals, contributing to up to 70% increases in experiences of fairness, respect, value, belonging, psychological safety, and inspiration.[8]

Therefore, it is insufficient to allow for age and gender diversity to maximize connectivity; families must also allow for inclusivity, by moving from being technically oriented to being relationally oriented.

The Features of Connected Families

In summary, connected families enjoy the 3Cs: they have clarity of vision, mission, and conviction, they communicate, and they collaborate well:

- They have independent family members yet are interdependent, and prioritize the good of the collective as well as the individual.
- They are connected vertically and horizontally and enjoy age and gender inclusion.

- They are united, not uniform.
- They see, hear, and deposit value to each other, as individuals feel seen, heard, and valued.
- Individuals belong, rather than fit in.
- The family provides a range of support (emotional, esteem, network, informational, and financial) to family members. They also draw on support from a range of family members at times of need.

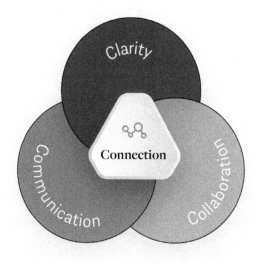

Consequently, connected families have an emotional bank with healthy deposits of trust and loyalty. This high level of internal connectivity within the family provides great external strength. This external strength provides resilience to withstand threats. In other words, connected families enjoy that Circle of Safety coined by Simon Sinek. This Circle of Safety is analogous to a security fence that wards off unwanted threats. When faced with disruptive circumstances, the family is able to withstand such, survive, and even thrive, as the fence provides a barrier.

As Simon Sinek explains, "Only when we feel we are in a Circle of Safety will we pull together as a unified team, better able to survive and thrive regardless of the conditions outside." Connected families are better able to survive and thrive regardless of the external conditions they face due to their internal connectivity.

CHAPTER 5

The Challenge for Founders

few years ago, I had the pleasure of coaching a next gen into a CEO role. Her father, founder of the family business, had decided to retire, and made himself accountable to both the family, the enterprise, and the wider community. They threw a send-off party to celebrate his accolades over the years and Dad was to move on to the next phase of his life, focusing on starting a new business. However, he struggled with moving on. He would still come into the office every day, wearing his suit, talking to the employees, and meddling in decisions that his daughter had made. This frustrated and embarrassed her; she couldn't understand why he could not accept this new chapter of his life after having publicly celebrated his retirement. She couldn't understand why he simply could not let go.

This is commonplace. For a founder who has become accustomed to coming into the business every day for decades, the finality of their exit from the business can be quite challenging.

This reminds me of my childhood. I loved rollercoasters—the thrill of the ride would give me dopamine highs for days! My dad also loved rides and he would take my siblings, my cousins, and me to theme parks during our summers. There was a particular theme park I loved to go to in England called Alton Towers. Alton Towers has a crazy ride called Oblivion, which was the world's first vertical drop rollercoaster where one literally drops vertically for 180 feet. It's a very short ride, but there's a lot of anticipation built into the experience. You rise to the top of the drop, and you are hanging on the edge for what feels like a lifetime! Suddenly you hear a voice say, "Don't look down!" as the drop into Oblivion is imminent. Then, WHOOSH, the drop happens and the whole thing is over within 15 seconds!

What I always found fascinating was that the fear and anxiety as we anticipated the drop was always worse than the experience of the drop itself (which was actually good fun)!

Leading psychologist Dr. Susan David describes this phenomenon as "betwixt," meaning "the anxiety of in-betweenness." Many founders are betwixt, plagued by transitional anxiety.

Anxiety and Retirement

The anxiety of being betwixt can defer or frustrate the retirement process. The founder may have made promises to family and staff to retire but find themselves continually pushing back the date, thereby frustrating others. Or, like my former client's father, they may retire and return; unable to truly retire, they hover over their businesses, holding on to control.

What is it about retiring that causes such transitional anxiety? Retirement is something that most founders do not actually want, but it is expected of them! Many feel that this expectation is imposed by society, employees, and their loved ones. Jeffrey Sonnenfeld conducted research looking at family business CEOs and their attitudes toward retirement. He found that many founders never intended to retire, nor did they look forward to it. They would consider retirement only in cases of poor health, boredom, or because one of their children was ready to take over. [9]

It would seem strange that founders do not want to retire—in society, retirement is generally seen as a hallmark event worth celebrating, as individuals move into the latter phase of their lives. The reason why many founders do not want to retire is that for them working is more than an occupation; it has a deeply personal meaning.

A few years ago, I met up with my mentor for coffee and needed guidance. I was working in corporate London at the time and had been put on an amazing project at work. It was a great opportunity to raise my profile in the department. But it was a complex project, and I found it quite challenging. Instead of starting, I would procrastinate, finding 1,001 mundane things to do instead. I recognized that there was mental friction to get started but didn't know what to do.

My mentor asked me three powerful questions that gave me a mind shift. She said, "What happened?"

I replied, "I can't seem to get started on this project. I just keep procrastinating." Then she said, "What's the feeling attached to that?" I said, "Overwhelm, mental clutter." Then, "And what does it mean to you?"

Initially, I didn't understand what she was getting at, so I took some time to reflect.

I recognized that procrastination was not the issue. I had a fear of not being good enough and consequently being rejected. Until I addressed those fears, I would struggle to stop procrastinating. It taught me an invaluable lesson in life: how important it is to gain an understanding of the distinction between external observable events and their internal personal meanings. Oftentimes, like an iceberg, what is unobservable holds clues to the root issue at hand. Until we discover the root, there'll be no resolution.

Similarly, there is a distinction between the retirement of a founder, which is an external observable event, and the meaning that they attach to it. It is important to delve deeper to understand these personal meanings.

The Emotional Challenge of Retiring

For a founder, retirement represents more than a loss of an occupation; it has deeply personal meanings.

1. The letting go of a child

Founders are like parents that have nurtured their babies from birth, to adolescence, to adulthood. The business is like a labor of love that has received their devotion of time, energy, and money. This concept of the business being the founder's child is more than a metaphor—it is backed by science. The results of a 2019 study[10] demonstrated that when entrepreneurs think about their businesses, their brain patterns are very similar to those of parents thinking about their children. When presented with pictures of their businesses or children, the researchers report a significant increase in activity of the parts of the brain associated with parenting, pleasant sensations, and rewards.

These strong emotional bonds explain why it is so difficult for a founder to let go: the emotional turmoil which they feel is similar to the grief that empty nesters feel when their children leave home. Just as empty nesters experience loss of identity as parents and loss of significance to their children, similarly the thought of letting go of their enterprises plagues founders with similar losses: they are grieving. For both empty nesters and retiring founders, the loneliness felt in grief compounds these negative emotions: the grief of empty nest syndrome is often not recognized, as it is considered normal for an adult child to move out of home. Similarly, the grief of letting go of one's business is often not recognized, as it is considered normal for an adult to retire.

2. The acknowledgement of their mortality

In addition, retiring means the acknowledgement of one's mortality. Retirement is simply a signpost for the aging process, and founders become increasingly aware of their mortality (mortality salience) with age. Psychologists often say that humans have a deep fear of death. This salience can be difficult to navigate. Terror management theory posits that increasing mortality salience leads to terror and anxiety.[11]

Sigmund Freud said, "It is true that the statement 'all men are mortal' is paraded in textbooks of logic as an example of a general proposition; but no human being really grasps it, and our unconscious has as little use now as it ever had for the idea of its own mortality."

Founders increasingly become aware of their mortality with age, but don't know what to do with that information. As a result, many deal with it by denial, by suppression of thoughts, or overestimating the time they have left, thereby frustrating the succession planning process.

3. Giving up of their tribe

Retirement not only means the acknowledgement of a founder's mortality, it also means the giving up of their tribe. Founders have carefully nurtured their businesses for decades. Oftentimes they are workaholics; their only hobby is the business. Therefore, their main social outlet is this tribe of employees, suppliers, customers, and community members. Retirement means giving up their carefully curated place of belonging.

Belonging is a fundamental human need: a study by Macdonald and Leary illustrates how humans experience physical pain when they feel socially excluded. A study on stressful life events ranked retirement as one of the most stressful life events, up to 50% more stressful than changes in financial status or the death of a close friend.[12] So anticipating the loss of one's tribe physically hurts.

4. The letting go of a calling

Lastly, retirement means letting go of their calling. In his book, The Hero's Farewell: What Happens When CEOs Retire, Jeffrey Sonnenfeld explains that many founders are likened to heroes on a mission to achieve legacy. Work is more than a job;

it is a calling. As a result, their exits from their businesses can be emotionally challenging, particularly where they feel that they have not had the opportunity to make the impact that they desire. Many business founders are type-A personalities who are high achievers and have a strong drive to leave a legacy. As they age, they may have bigger goals, so instead of letting go of the enterprise, they hold on tighter. The letting go of their calling is a loss of significance.

Managing the Transition

Founders are anticipating many losses: loss of a child, the loss of their existence, loss of their tribe, and the loss of their calling. They are grieving, and their grief requires witnessing. Oftentimes, other family members are unaware of their emotional turmoil, and this can make them isolated rather than connected.

Connection is necessary for managing this transition successfully as it yields dependency and support. To move past grief, the bereaved need to feel seen, loved, and not alone. As David Kessler says, "Grief requires witnessing," but founders find themselves being celebrated for their transition instead of being comforted in their pain. Consequently, it's difficult for them to heal when their loss is not recognized.

Just as connection to others is key to managing traditional grief, connection to family members helps founders transition to their latter stage of life. In addition to the emotional support it provides, connection allows for intellectual support. Founders are grappling with many complex decisions to make, including what's next—for themselves as individuals, and for their businesses. Connection enables diversity of thought to bring about the best quantity and quality of ideas, establishing greater clarity.

CHAPTER 6

Challenges the Rising Generation Face

t is often said that values are caught and not taught, meaning that values are often learned by seeing them practiced, rather than being explained. Most founders are high-achieving type-A personalities who are highly ambitious. Oftentimes, next gens have "caught" this value of achievement, ambition, and accomplishment, and wish to take the family enterprise to greater heights. But the unwillingness of the wealth creators to relinquish control gets in the way, and next gens feel unable to rise to their potential and maximize their impact on the family enterprise.

Back to my former client: she had expressed frustration about being the new CEO. Employees, suppliers, and customers perceived her as being in the decision-making seat, but in reality she felt like a puppet: Dad was still calling the shots and interfering in her decision-making. The juxtaposition of the perception of others and her lived reality of feeling bound was really frustrating. Originally from Kenya, her parents had sent her to boarding school in Switzerland at the age of 13. Thereafter, she studied for an undergraduate degree in the U.K. and a postgraduate degree in the States. After her post-graduate degree, she worked in New York in an investment bank. She felt that both her education, global exposure, and work experience meant she had a lot to offer the family business, but her father's seeming reluctance to let go was stifling her ability to make an impact. He was not giving her sufficient room to "grab on."

A lot of next gens face similar challenges: a consequence of founders not letting go is that it becomes difficult for next gens to grab on. Many feel they are not given sufficient room to make a stamp on the family enterprise. Like my client, many next gens may enjoy formal leadership roles and titles, but they often cite a lack of authority: for example, 67% of next gens currently play an active role in their family office, while 24% serve in leadership roles in their family businesses, but 22% cite that the wealth holder is unwilling to relinquish control.[13] Navigating this tension between de-jure power and de facto lack of authority can be very frustrating for next gens.

The Invisibility of Inaudibility

Next gens often describe feeling "invisible," as their voices are not being heard. They can't get a word in! The duality of not being seen and heard is a challenge. Author Gip Roberts describes invisibility as being a "curse" and explains that there is more than one way to be invisible. To quote:

Invisibility is not always all about physical transparency. In my case, it's about a combination of factors. Some of them physical. Some of them abstract. It's about all five of the senses: what people see, what they hear, what they smell, what they feel, and what they think."

Being inaudible can contribute to feeling invisible. This duality of invisibility and inaudibility is particularly challenging because, as human beings, we all have a desire to be both seen and heard. However, next gens often aren't. They would love to have their voices heard in areas where they believe they can add value, namely professionalizing, digitizing, technology, innovation, attracting and retaining talent, diversity and inclusion, and sustainability.

Yearning for Help

According to the PWC Global Next Gen 2019 Survey, many cite needing assistance in unlocking their potential so that they can meet their goals. Many successors are high achieving like their parents; however, unlike their parents, they are often insecure about their ability to make money. They have not started a business from inception, turning water into wine. They often feel insignificant compared to their parents who seem to have amazing entrepreneurial instincts.

As a result of this insecurity, many next gens desire to be guided, coached, and mentored in a structured way. The challenge is that their parents are often not ones for structure! In

Wickman and Winters' book Rocket Fuel, the authors explain that businesses need a combination of two distinct types of leaders to "take off." They explain that businesses need both a visionary and an integrator. A visionary has ideas and a powerful imagination, sees visions, and has unusual foresight. An integrator unites the major functions of the business, keeps the trains running on time, and creates accountability and alignment. Visionaries have the entrepreneurial spirit to seize opportunities and dream big, whereas integrators are administrators, aligning resources to make the visionary's dream a reality.

Many founders are visionaries. As a result, they typically make decisions based on intuition, rather than data. They continuously get new ideas, and their "genius" is in their head and heart. Whereas many next gens are integrators; they seek process, systems, and procedures. Consequently, founders find it difficult to provide structured learning for their successors, as there is no structure to their genius! They would encourage others to learn on the job. Next gens, on the other hand, feel that on-the-job learning is ineffective; they may have observed decisions being made but do not necessarily understand the process the founder went through in arriving at decisions. This can make the rising generation insecure about their potential to lead.

I recall meeting a second-generation family business leader who was thoroughly frustrated with his father. Though the son was appointed general manager of the family business, he felt completely disempowered due to his father's reluctance to let go. After complaining about several strategic decisions he disagreed with his father on, he proceeded to share his insecurities.

He said, "I don't even know if there's a method to this madness. I can't say categorically whether my ideas would work or not." This insecurity is frequently shared by those who feel like they have not yet practiced their leadership.

Being Stuck Backstage

A couple of years ago, my husband and I saw Fela and the Kalakuta Queens, an amazing show chronicling the life of Fela Anikulapo Kuti, a Nigerian musician and political activist, and his 28 wives. I was captivated by the music, the wardrobe, the lighting, and the actors onstage. It was a well-coordinated production where the actors brought the characters to life and thoroughly entertained us. After the show, I went backstage, and saw many people behind the scenes who had contributed toward this excellent production. It dawned on me that while those who were working backstage were critical in ensuring the successful running of the show, they were not substitutable for those working onstage.

If the director were to suggest that the sound technician substitute for the lead actor, he would likely be plagued with anxiety. He may think, "Am I good enough to play this role without sufficient practice?" I realized that intergenerational leadership in family enterprises has similar parallels: many next gens feel like they are currently backstage. However, they are anxious that they will be thrust frontstage with minimal notice. Instead, they wish to master their leadership competence through repeated rehearsing.

Living in the Shadow of Wealth

Another commonly observed challenge that next gens face is living in the shadow of their parents' wealth. Many feel that they do not have a right to own the wealth, as they did not earn it legitimately. This leads to them developing complex identities toward wealth. This is worsened by the fact that our society frequently shames wealth.

Not only does society frequently shame wealth, it also particularly shames inherited wealth: the connotation is that inheritors are somewhat less than wealth creators, and so inherited wealth often evokes envy and resentment among the public. Eric J. Shoenberg, a psychologist from Columbia University, explains, "Society is wary of the wealth that inheritors receive without any effort on their own part. Society accepts the legitimacy of the inheritor's wealth, but questions the status that normally accompanies that wealth." [14]

Furthermore, talking about money remains taboo. As such, it is difficult for families of wealth to have conversations about the emotions around wealth. This can leave next gens feeling lonely and confused about their identity toward it.

They may also feel like it is an obstacle to having authentic relationships: "Are they trying to befriend me for me or because of my wealth?" they often ask themselves. Female inheritors in particular tend to struggle with feeling like their wealth is an obstacle to potential romantic relationships. A lot of this is due to societal conditioning around traditional gender roles in relationships, where males are to be the providers and females are to be the nurturers. Inheriting significant wealth as a woman therefore narrows the pool of potential men, as society expects women to "marry up," and discourages them from "marrying down."

Furthermore, the historical pattern of wealth transfers plays a role: in the 1900s, fathers typically bequeathed to their daughters one half of the share to their sons, and gave control of their daughters' shares to their sons.[15] In contrast, 2022 exhibits rapidly growing wealth inheritance by women. According to Barclays Private Bank, "More than 60% of the UK's wealth is expected to be in women's hands by 2025." Furthermore, it is estimated that most of the private wealth is likely to be transferred to women over the coming decades. Despite this changing tide, a lot of women have internalized external gender narratives, such that they are distanced, disconnected, and have dysfunction toward ownership and management of wealth. As such, many resent it, feeling like prisoners of their circumstances rather than empowered by privilege.

Stewardship Anxiety

The 2020 Campden Wealth Survey found that more than 54% of next gens are worried that they will lose the wealth the family has created. Furthermore, 62% feel it is their responsibility to not only preserve, but also grow their family wealth. [16] As explained, next gens are often high achievers, and they feel a subconscious pressure to "outdo" the former generation. Sayings like "May the ceiling of this generation be the floor of the next" may be etched in their minds and put them under immense pressure.

As a result, many frequently cite a feeling of stewardship anxiety, where they have a deep fear of incompetence to not only preserve all that has been built, but to also grow it and pass it on to the next generation. This anxiety is compounded by the fact that many feel like they have not been given sufficient room to practice their leadership, and do not even know whether they are competent enough to do so. Their lack of authority and control in the family enterprise contributes to a feeling of disempowerment. This dichotomy is stressful and is a heavy emotional cross to bear.

The rising generation face complex challenges as they anticipate the torch being passed over to their generation. Many feel that their voices are not being heard and that they have not been given room to practice their leadership. They desire greater support to unlock their potential so that they can be more effective change champions in their family enterprises. In addition to these leadership struggles, many struggle with emotional challenges associated with their identity and fears toward wealth. As a result, many next gens are lonely and feel misunderstood as they lack safe spaces to discuss these complex issues.

Like founders, next gens also need connection: they need a safe space to discover and develop their unique leadership; they need a safe space to process their emotions surrounding wealth. Further, they need a safe space to connect with their siblings. By forming a common vision and voice on family enterprise matters, they become more effective catalysts for change with their parents.

CHAPTER 7

Generational Attitudes

A common reason for disconnect, dysfunction, and distance in family firms is differences in generational attitudes. As an ardent champion of diversity, I feel slightly nauseous when I am forced to make generalisations about people based on age, gender, race, etc., because I am of the strong opinion that we are all authors of our lives; we hold the pen and write the script to shape our futures. Like Nilofer Merchant, I believe in "The Power of Onlyness": each of us occupies a spot in the world where we uniquely stand, which is a function of our unique histories, experiences, visions, and hopes, and when we tap into this onlyness, we can become unstoppable forces for good in our world.

That being said, while I believe that our power is not determined by our demographic, we are shaped by our demographics. So the study of generational trends has a place, giving us critical perspectives and helping us to relate better with one another.

Generational Lenses

Leading entrepreneur, historian, and best-selling author, Fawn Weaver said, "I've noticed the most challenging part of most people's lives is not reality, it's their perception of reality—their own self-made movie. As the director of my own film, I get to decide by what lens I will view myself, the world, and those around you. What's your camera lens?"

Getting into the habit of asking this question both for ourselves and for others is powerful; there is no objective reality, only a subjective one. Through that camera lens, we see our own reality. Two individuals can experience the same event and have two unique subjective realities. Age strongly influences one's lens, as age determines common history, both inherited and lived. Just as our individual histories shape how we see our present and future, similarly our collective histories also shape how we see our present and future. The implication of this is that unique subjective realities can create divergence in perspectives as a result of age/generations, resulting in differences in generational lenses.

Furthermore, different social groups vary in how they remember their shared past. For example, Americans' memory of World War II differs drastically from that of the Russians': Americans would often cite Pearl Harbor, D-Day, and the Hiroshima and Nagasaki bombings as critical markers of the war, whereas Russians would cite the Battle of Stalingrad and the Battle of Kursk. Russians do not even refer to the war as World War II; they call it The Great Patriotic War. If social groups differ in both their memory of their shared pasts and their labeling of their shared pasts, their awareness of their present and perspectives of their futures are bound to vary too.

Boomers Versus Millennials

In family enterprises, most founders are baby boomers. On the other hand, most second-generation family members are millennials. Boomers are typically characterized by being "Confident, self-reliant, goal-oriented and career focused," whereas millennials have "High expectations of their employers, seek new challenges at work and are unafraid to question authority." [17] These differing generational lenses can lead to disconnection, distance, and dysfunction.

Baby boomers were born between 1946 and 1964, and were greatly influenced by a post-World War II world. Globally, the boomers saw drastic social revolutions in the 1960s, including civil rights and women's rights movements. They typically came of age at a time of increasing affluence and opportunity. In Africa, many boomers were born during seasons of huge political transition, an era of post-colonial Africa, and many lived through their nations gaining independence from their colonial masters. They had a sense of optimism toward the future of their nations, as opportunities became increasingly available to "indigenes."

However, it wasn't all roses; many boomers in Africa experienced volatile economies. Living in mainly commodity-driven nations, they experienced periods of immense economic booms as well as drastic recessions.

Millennials were born between 1981 and 1996 and were greatly influenced by a world characterized by increasing connectivity through technology and social media. Coined the "digital native" generation, millennials came of age during the rise of the internet. Consequently, their perception of the world and relationships with others was greatly shaped by access to information. Significant events affecting this generation include global terrorism, and the Great Financial Crash in 2008, which coincided with the time that many were seeking their first jobs.

Millennials are a generation who distrusts traditional institutions. According to a 2015 poll by Harvard University's Institute of Politics, of ten societal institutions, millennials only trust two: the military and scientists. This has huge implications as it means this generation does not trust government, business, religious bodies, the media, and law enforcement bodies. So … what or whom do they trust? Information from their devices!

Their connection to their devices has meant that millennials have grown up in a much more connective, connected world than their parents: this has widened their worldview to a much more global one than that of their parents. In Africa, many next gens are bicultural—they may have been raised in their countries of origin, but often they're sent to the West for secondary and/or tertiary education. Many choose to settle and remain in the West. Others return to their country of origin. Despite their choice of location, many straddle two contrasting cultures, a collectivist African culture and an individualist Western one.

Clashing Leadership Perspectives

The digital native generations may seek to do things in a new way: they've lived through the Information Age and have a knack for all things innovation, technology, and digitalisation. They may seek to future-proof their family enterprises in the way that is native to them; 61% of next gens say that technology is one of the three most important drivers of change.[18] They may face resistance from the boomers, whose generation succeeded through growth in the "real economy," (i.e. manufacturing, real estate, infrastructure, and agriculture) and are nervous about change.

In addition, the changing societal values over generations can be a challenge. Since the rising generation has been exposed to Western cultures that promote autonomy, independence, and critical thinking, they may not feel a sense of duty and obligation to return to the family enterprise and take over operational leadership from Mom or Dad. They may choose to stay in the West and forge their own paths, while Mom or Dad are perplexed as to how to take the business forward when their children take no interest in taking over.

This distinct emerging generation has challenged the status quo on the purpose of business; sticklers for conscious capitalism, they want to see organizations that not only generate profits, but have meaningful purposes—businesses that would be a force for good. On the other hand, boomers traditionally separated their profit activities from their social activities, through corporate social responsibility and/or philanthropic activities. The rising generation is challenging their parents on their business models, seeking to see a greater integration of social change in their traditional business models through social entrepreneurship, sustainable philanthropy, and impact investing.

Millennials are also known as the social media generation, and are quick to be opinionated and outspoken through social media. Many members of the rising generation are passionate about social issues surrounding diversity, inclusion, equity, social justice, and climate change, and are typically quite outspoken about their views online. They also expect businesses to communicate their values through their online presence. Baby boomers, on the other hand, tend to be more discreet with their use of social media, typically concerned about the impact of such on the family's reputation and brand.

Time Perspectives

Another reason for the disconnection, distance, and dysfunction across generations is time orientation. As individuals, we have different predispositions to our orientation to time, and these tend to evolve with age. The three sets of time perspectives are past-oriented, present-oriented, or future-oriented as identified by leading psychologist Philip Zimbardo. Past-oriented people primarily focus on the past, and value the old more than the new, value the familiar over the novel, and value the conservative approach over the risky. Present-oriented people are largely driven by what is happening now: they are driven by their impulses and typically do not plan. Future-oriented people tend to look and plan ahead.

Most of us start off life present-focused: no baby comes into the world with a plan. Instead, they are largely in pursuit of pleasure rather than pain. As we develop into young adults, we tend to be future-focused and as we develop into more mature adults, we tend to be past-oriented, reminiscing on the past and seeking to preserve history and rituals.

Zimbardo explains how critical an understanding of time perspectives is. He says:

> *Many of life's puzzles can be solved by simply understanding our own time perspective and that of others. Lots of conflict we have with people is really a conflict in the different time perspectives. Once you're aware of that you stop making negative attributions like, you're dumb or you're childish or you're pig-headed or you're authoritarian. It's really the most simple idea in the world."*

The implication of this in a family enterprise is that our different time perspectives affect investment horizon, business strategic outlook, risk appetite, value systems, and family strategic outlook. Founders tend to be focused on history, heritage, and values, whereas next gens tend to be itching for change—seeking innovation, use of technology, and professionalization. It is therefore possible that a business decision that is optimal for someone who is present-oriented may be detrimental for one who is future-oriented. It is important to connect the generations because we want a healthy balance of past-, present-, and future-oriented family members when making decisions.

This is because each time orientation has its downsides: past-oriented business leaders would resist change and innovation. They would hold on to heritage and tradition. They may find themselves obliterated by disruption. Present-oriented business leaders may not have a strategic plan for the business and/or the family, and may be improvising. This can limit the potential longevity of the business and/or the wealth. Lastly, future-oriented business leaders may have greater risk appetites for business/investment decisions. This can result in the family being asset-rich but cash-poor today.

Time Priorities

Differing life stages can also contribute toward multigenerational clashes in family firms. Psychologist Erik Erikson developed a theory on the life stages of psychosocial development. He believed that personality developed in eight stages, and that in each stage, people experience a conflict.

A summary of the eight stages is shown in the diagram below:[19]

According to Erikson's theory, those between the ages of 19 and 40 fall into the Young Adulthood Stage. Therefore, most next gens would fall here. At this stage of development, young adults desire close, committed, loving relationships with others.

They desire intimacy. In addition to craving connection, young adults desire independence.

Those between the ages of 40 and 65 would be in the Middle Adulthood Stage, where most founders would be. At this stage, adults desire generativity; the major question on their minds is, "How can I contribute to the world?" They have a desire to create things that will outlast them, through their children or through creating a change that has a positive impact on people and community. They desire to leave a legacy. At this age, founders are usually plagued by fear that time to make this impact and leave a legacy is running out.

Life stage clashes can therefore have dysfunctional effects in a family enterprise. Research by John Davis of the University of Southern California corroborates this theory that life clashes between parent and child can exacerbate tensions in transitions.[20] This is because next gens are striving for independence, autonomy, and a greater voice in the family enterprise, during a time when founders are running to make an impact against a ticking clock.

Generational analyses are important in a family firm, as one's age remains one of the greatest predictors of one's preferences, priorities, and perspectives.[20]

In a family, it is key to gain understanding of each other's preferences, priorities, and perspectives, as this lack of understanding can hinder collaboration, communication, and collective clarity, critical tenets required for families to be connected. It is on a foundation of connectedness that a legacy enterprise is built.

CHAPTER 8

Nuances of Family Businesses

amily businesses by their very nature are more complicated than non-family firms. These two institutions—family and business—often have opposing objectives. For example, the family system is a unit that is to provide unconditional love, psychological safety, and nurturing for family members, whereas the business system is one that is to provide a return on investment for stakeholders, and its employees are measured by performance, productivity, and profitability.

Another way to think of this is to consider family and business as two different sports. To win any sport, you must be aware of the rules and apply them appropriately. For instance, in soccer, the objective of the game is to kick the ball into the net, whereas in basketball the objective of the game is to throw the ball through the hoop. If a basketball player kicks the ball or a soccer player throws the ball, they are disqualified from the game and are penalized. Similarly, if you apply the rules of the family game to the business sphere, and vice versa, you set yourself up to lose the game and create conflict among your teammates.

An example of this is below:

> *Tolu is 25 and has just returned to Nigeria from
> the U.K. after studying his masters and working in
> financial services for a few years. He starts working in
> the family business as Executive Director—Corporate
> Services. The general manager, Chudi, a long-
> standing non-family staff that has been with the
> business for 20 years, now reports to Tolu. Chudi
> watched Tolu grow up. In fact, Chudi used to prepare
> the bank instructions for Jimi, Tolu's father, to move
> money to him for his school fees, so he feels like he
> raised Tolu also.*

> *Tolu's returning to the business has left a bad taste
> in Chudi's mouth as Tolu is earning three times
> what Chudi is, despite having been at the business
> longer. Chudi is becoming resentful, and his morale
> is depleted on the daily. He perceives that there's
> a ceiling in the business—Tolu is on the path to
> successor. What's the point? Chudi is now considering
> jumping ship to an environment where he perceives
> there are better opportunities for him.*

In this example, Jimi, Tolu's father, is applying the rules of family to the business realm. As a father, he wants to ensure that his son is adequately provided for. However, in the business realm, to score a goal one must be focused on rewarding employees based on merit, not sentiment. Consequently, he stands to potentially lose a long-standing staff member who has a lot of institutional memory, as a result of neglecting the rules of the business game. Families are often weighed down by such clashes.

The Tension Between Priorities

In addition to their opposing "rules," the confluence of these two institutions gives rise to additional complexity. This is because the size and nature of the overlap is a variable, giving rise to a myriad of combinations and permutations. Does your family prioritize the business needs or prioritize the family's needs? Do these needs change over time? These choices depend on your family.

The tension between family and business can be difficult to reconcile.

An example of this is working moms, who often have the "working mom dilemma";[21] they feel guilty for being away from the home while at work, and feel guilty for being away from work while at home. The result is that this guilt gets in their way of being present both at home and at work, affects their mood, and has a negative effect on their productivity. Ultimately, both their personal and professional lives suffer.

Similarly, many family business owners are plagued by the family business dilemma: in constantly weighing up the tensions between family and business in absence of clarity, business owners are unable to optimize decision-making for both the family and business units.

This need not be; just as working moms can set themselves up to thrive both at home and work, family business owners can navigate the tensions between family and business such that both units thrive.

One of my favorite sheroes, Brené Brown, is a thought leader and influencer on all things vulnerability and daring leadership. In the middle of the COVID-19 pandemic, I found myself both exhilarated and petrified about the known unknowns and unknown unknowns in my personal life, family life, and business life. I was in a season of fragility, juxtaposed against possibility: in one breath, the global pandemic was caving in on me, having evolved from a public health crisis to an economic crisis to personal tragedies in my life; and in another, many opportunities were opening up. Brown's podcast *Unleashing Us* was my crux for inspiration and mind makeovers.

In one episode, Brown spoke about the phenomenon of tensions in opposite, and how such tensions contribute to stress. She explained that a lot of us may be straddling tensions of opposites, i.e. holding many contradictory pieces and feelings. Her reassurance was that not only are tensions and contradictory pieces okay and normal, they're also the magic sauce.

Tensions in and of themselves are not necessarily bad; they can be our winning edge, our magic sauce of sorts. However, for tensions to be our winning edge, they need to be reconciled. Indeed, the very tensions between family and business can become magic sauce, a source of unrivaled competitive advantage.

The Challenge of Change

In addition to the inherent conflicts between family and business at any given point in time, you may find that you are navigating simultaneous change at three different levels: individual, family, and business. As you are seeking to transition from generation one to generation two, you have to navigate change at these multiple micro levels, to bring about change at the macro family enterprise level.

It is like gears in a car: the individual micro units are like the wheels that spin independently; however, the interaction of their movements, their interdependence, determines the overall speed of the car. Similarly, the individual, family, and business units are changing independently, as well as interdependently, and this influences the overall family enterprise. The key individuals in the family enterprise include the family members, key staff, other shareholders, and board members. For the purpose of this analysis, I will focus on the family members.

The Importance of Story

Each family member is going through their individual stage of their personal life: these include childhood, puberty, adolescence, adulthood, middle age, and the senior years. In addition to these common stages of life, each individual goes through their "life chapters." It is often said that life is like a book comprised of various chapters. We go through different experiences in life that are like stories.

I lived in Lagos, Nigeria for the first half of my childhood. I hated English Comprehension in primary school, and I really struggled to pay attention and listen to stories. My teacher, Mrs. Eke, who ruled with an iron fist, was intimidating both in size and in presence. She would read us a story, and then pick us at random and ask, "What is the moral of the story?" I often wondered why it mattered, it was all make-believe anyway, and I would make up the answers when asked. Mrs. Eke would scold me and tell me to pay closer attention. It wasn't until I grew older that I learnt that Mrs. Eke was instilling in me a critical life skill: to always ask myself, "What is the moral of this story?"

In the family enterprise, each individual goes through a journey, and this journey is shaped by their story and the meaning they attach to it. Arguably, one's life chapters are more important than one's life stages. It is in asking of oneself "What is the moral of this story" that one learns more about oneself, one's world, and one's purpose.

The Growing Complexity of Generations

The family unit is also subject to change. The family unit grows more complex over generations. Typically, it grows exponentially over time. The rising generation typically settle down with partners and have children, leading to a larger family through new births, as well as a more complicated family through marriages (new clans, tribes, and factions). Families also have to grapple with the loss of family members through deaths, separations, and/or divorces. In addition, our 21st century reality is that families are increasingly geographically dispersed. This means that families become increasingly influenced by multiple cultures.

For example, I lived in Lagos until I was nine. Thereafter, my family moved to the U.K. for the rest of my childhood and early adulthood. My siblings and I had a different world view to our parents, shaped by the strong influence of British culture. I remember feeling like I was straddling two worlds, the Nigerian world at home, and the British world outside of our doorstep, and feeling like I did not belong in either.

Your family may be in a similar situation, straddling multiple cultures. You may see a clash of values between different generations as the family works to collectively discover itself.

These nuances make family businesses more complex than non-family firms due to the competing objectives of family and business, and the simultaneous changes families are navigating on individual, family, and personal levels, as well as the growing complexity across generations. As a result, legacy businesses are not achieved without intentionality.

Legacies are not built overnight: like a farmer sowing a seed, building a legacy requires intentionality. It does not happen by osmosis! It requires consistency in carefully cultivating, watering, and nurturing the seed so that it reaches its fullest potential. With appropriate long-term planning, families can overcome these obstacles to legacy.

CHAPTER 9

Embracing the Transition

To navigate change at every level and embrace transition amidst the nuance of the family business, the founder needs to switch from being a boss to being a mentor to the siblings, while the rising generation members move from students to leaders in their own right. The siblings also need to transition from independence to greater levels of interdependence, as they will be leading collectively.

These adjustments are challenging. Not only is the founder dealing with grief and anxiety and as such finds it difficult to adjust, but also the siblings tend to find it difficult to form a team. Their effective working together and productive decision-making does not happen by osmosis.

This is because team formation takes intentionality and time. Teams often go through stages of development as identified by Bruce Tuckman, an educational psychologist. These stages include forming, storming, norming, performing, and adjourning.

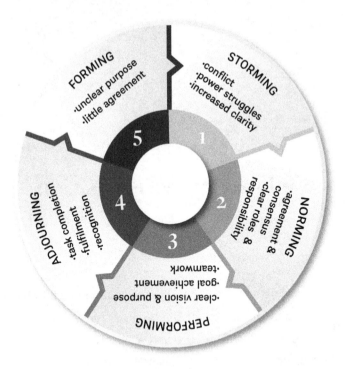

The diagram shows a circular cycle with five segments:

FORMING
- unclear purpose
- little agreement

STORMING
- conflict
- power struggles
- increased clarity

NORMING
- agreement
- consensus
- clear roles & responsibility

PERFORMING
- clear vision & purpose
- goal achievement
- teamwork

ADJOURNING
- task completion
- fulfilment
- recognition

Inner numbers: 5, 1, 2, 3, 4

⍦ Forming: This is a period of acquaintance and orientation. While the rising generation members may know each other as siblings, they will need to get to know each other as business partners. They may have never worked together. At this stage, they get to know each other's strengths and weaknesses, their expectations and their roles.

⍦ Storming: This is the most challenging stage, where there is a lot of conflict and competition as individuals show their personalities. As a result, performance may fall due to lack of alignment on goals, values, vision, and mission. Team performance is lowest at this stage. To proceed, siblings need to work on shared tasks and goals, accept differences, and look to overcome obstacles.

- Norming: Here the storm is over, and some semblance of normalcy resumes. The siblings have a degree of cohesion and oneness. At this stage they start to have consensus on their individual roles, and who will be a leader. They have an understanding of acceptable behaviors and what level of performance is acceptable. Team performance rises as siblings learn to collaborate and work toward a common goal. However, disagreements can pull the team back into storming stage, where conflict is rife and performance falls.

- Performing: Here the siblings have formed consensus and can collaborate effectively. They are organized and well functioning. They have a good structure and commitment to the team vision, mission, and goals. Conflicts may arise but are dealt with. Performance is highest at this stage.

- Adjourning: Here the siblings' goals have been met. Perhaps they are passing on the responsibility to the cousin consortium or they decide to go their separate ways. They spend their time on wrapping up and documenting their work.

Obstacles to Team Formation

Unfortunately, siblings oftentimes have not started the formation of their team prior to the death of the founder. So they are forced to begin forming and storming during a crisis moment (i.e. the death of their parent).

Grief sears. It leaves an indelible mark on the bereaved: it isolates, altering one's mood, perspective, and emotions such that it is difficult to connect with others, let alone form a team.

No ordinary team at that! A team that is tasked with important work that has high stakes: leadership of a business and assets that represent an accumulation of decades of blood, sweat, and tears. The pressure to steward is on, and as such the decisions made need to have a high impact. Conflict may emerge as different siblings air their views and show their personalities. Long-standing sibling rivalries may become apparent.

The combination of grief, high stakes, and incessant conflict can make it difficult for siblings to norm. Many siblings find themselves stuck at storming for many years as they squabble and bicker. The storm becomes their norm. The conflict can lead to the demise of the enterprise, as performance drops. To optimize team performance, the siblings need to work on shared tasks and goals, accepting differences and looking to overcome obstacles as they move into norming.

The business unit is also subject to change. It is like a baby that grows into an infant, teen, and adult. Just as when a baby is born and experiences the fastest rate of growth and development in its first year of life than the rest of its life, similarly, when a business is established, it typically sees rapid growth of revenue, cash, and profitability in the early years. Over time, the child grows less quickly. Similarly, after a generation, the business grows less quickly, as it moves into a season of maturity. In this season, it may experience slowdown of revenues, cash, and profitability. This can be a challenge for business families, as this typically coincides with the added complexities and transitions in the family. The rate of growth of the family is larger than the rate of growth of the business. The "GDP per capita" of the business declines over time, and decision-making becomes more challenging as well. It can be harder to see an alignment within this larger, more complex family.

In addition, businesses must grapple with a disrupted industry landscape. Family enterprises are facing a 21st century volatile, uncertain, complex, and ambiguous (VUCA) world that has disrupted business models and industries. We are seeing a rise of blockchain, artificial intelligence, big data, cloud, and mobile. Current business owners are having to grapple with an unprecedented rate of change that the prior generation did not have to go through. By 2030, one third of all jobs will require skills that don't currently exist today. The implications of this are that both business models and leadership styles need to adapt.

Business owners are also facing social challenges on a scale that no prior generation had to. The effects of climate change and income inequalities across the world present a great challenge for the next generation of leaders, who are saddled with seeking both financial returns on investment and social change, and must change their approach to achieve this.

These changes in the business require the family to be agile and adaptable, and can change their role toward the business, their leadership style, and their business model.

Throw a Third System Into the Mix

The classic Three Circle Model of the Family Business System developed by Renato Taguiri and John Davis in 1978 shows that family businesses are comprised of three underlying systems: family, business, and ownership.

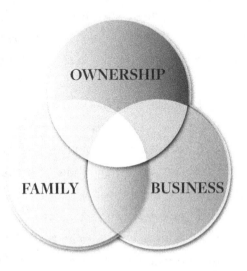

These three systems are interdependent. A family business is likened to an organism with constituent interrelated systems. A baby has underlying nervous, digestive, and respiratory systems, and the successful growth of the baby is determined by both the health of the individual systems and the ability for these systems to collaborate effectively with one another. Similarly, the successful growth of family businesses across generations is determined by both the health of the individual family, business, and ownership systems, and the ability for them to collaborate effectively with one another.

These systems also often overlap, as illustrated in the Venn diagram. As a result of the potential overlaps, there are seven possible roles/stakeholder groups formed by the underlying systems. As such an individual in a family business system may occupy up to seven potential stakeholder groups.

OWNERSHIP

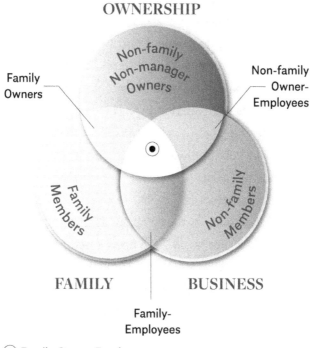

The seven different stakeholder groups that arise include:

1) Family members, not involved in the business, and are not owners;
2) Family members that are employed in the business but are not owners;
3) Family owners that are employed in the business;
4) Family owners that are not employed in the business;
5) Non-family employees;

6) Non-family owners who work in the business; and

7) Non-family owners who do not work in the business.

This model has significant implications for families. The first of which is that different stakeholder groups have different priorities, preferences, and perspectives.

Consider our example in Chapter 8 on Tolu and Chudi. Tolu is a family owner that is employed in the business. When Tolu was employed, he was not subjected to any hiring process, onboarding process, screening, or training. Tolu expects that his father will remunerate him sufficiently to cover his standard of living. He has no regard for the existing company Human Resources policies, processes, and procedures. The last few years have been a relatively challenging time for the company, as they lost a significant client. As a result, the family have been injecting funds into the business to support working capital. Tolu is looking forward to seeing the profitability of the business growing so that the shareholder loans can be repaid and he can finally receive a dividend.

On the other hand, Chudi is a non-family employee. When Chudi was hired, he was subjected to an interview. In addition, he is appraised biannually. Chudi has a wife and three and a half children. Chudi is the breadwinner to his growing family. He is under pressure to move to a nicer side of the city as his current neighborhood has been experiencing increasing crime. In addition, his three children are all in private school. The business has established a new business line to grow the revenue, and this has led to a significant increase in scope of Chudi's responsibilities. He is working longer hours for the same pay. He desires a salary increase so he can attend to his family's needs.

It is clear from our example that Tolu and Chudi have

different priorities, preferences, and perspectives when it comes to their respective relationships with the family business based on the fact that they are different stakeholder groups. Key to the success of the family business is understanding and addressing each stakeholder group's needs.

Ownership of the Business

Most of us understand what family and business refers to, but what is ownership? It refers to an investor role. For instance, one may have purchased $100 worth of Apple shares. As an investor, one is seeking to maximize the return on investment either through appreciation of the share price, or through dividend income. In addition as an investor, one is seeking that the risk profile of the shares is appropriate based on the investor's goals. In addition, one is seeking that the ownership structure of the shares is robust from a legal perspective, such that the owner can enforce ownership rights, through participating in Annual General Meetings and so forth.

In a family business, owners also have similar goals. Whilst in the example of Apple, ownership is passive, often in a family business environment, ownership is active. The owners of the business may have invested their savings to start it, and complemented their savings with bank loans. These bank loans may have been secured by their personal guarantees. The family business owners are wanting to maximize their returns on investment, either through dividends or the value of the business. They are also keen on ensuring that the bank loans are repaid appropriately so that their personal guarantees are not called. They also are keen to ensure that their wishes and desires for the company are enforceable through governance structures, for instance as board members.

Active ownership in a family enterprise often looks like:

- Providing equity and/or debt
- Enforcing voting rights to control equity decision through governance
- Mitigating the risks of the enterprise
- Strategic decision-making, e.g. new markets, new products, hiring executives, mergers, and acquisitions

Evolution Over Time

Families evolve over time: "In Generation to Generation: Life Cycles of the Family Business," Gersick et al. outline a model with Three Stages of Development of the Family Business. This model illustrates three stages of ownership.

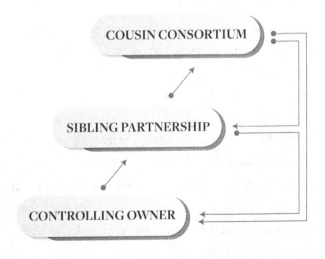

In generation one, typically families are at the "controlling owner"[22] stage, where the founder of the business is a parent, the president/CEO, and sole shareholder (or with his/her spouse). The founder is constantly juggling their identities (as a parent, business leader, and investor) both consciously and unconsciously. As the founder assumes these multiple identities simultaneously, they enjoy access to information from all systems and perform this owner role informally and intuitively. There is typically high levels of founder-centricity in the family and the business.

Moving from generation one to generation two, it gets more complicated. As explained earlier, the family gets larger and the enterprise evolves from being founder-led to being governed under a "siblings partnership."[23] Under a siblings partnership, the rising generation control the business together.

It is at this point where we see a divergence of the circles in the three-circle model, and greater diversity of the roles various family members occupy. Some family members may own shares and work in the business ("on the frontlines"), while others may own shares and not work in the business ("on the sidelines"). Over generations, we also tend to see greater geographic dispersion in the family: second generation family members may live in different parts of the world. This dispersion affects their proximity to the business and therefore information, and they also become multicultural in nature. Lastly, the business may be larger in size and more complex in make-up: there may be more operating businesses, shared assets, and philanthropic activities.

This divergence of circles, geographic locations, and evolution in scope of the family enterprise can contribute to a divergence of perspectives, and information asymmetry. For instance, those on the sidelines may feel that those working in the business are being too generously rewarded as employees, whereas those on the frontlines may feel that more funds should be used to reinvest in the business rather than paid out as dividends to owners.

There may be a clash of values as a result of the geographic dispersion: North America and European countries tend to highly value individualism, independence, and self-sufficiency, whereas Africa, Asia, the Middle East, and South America tend to highly value collectivism. In individualistic cultures, one is encouraged to be autonomous, to think independently and to challenge the status quo. In collectivist cultures, there's a greater emphasis on interdependency, cooperation, respect for hierarchies, and a premium on social standing. As a result of the above, it is necessary that families deliberately evolve from an informal owners' management to a formalized owners' management, to bring about diversity of thought rather than conflict.

Lastly, the increased complexity necessitates moving from the informal to the institutional: under the controlling owner, policies, procedures, and processes may not have been a priority, given the high founder-centricity. In contrast, given the higher levels of complexity, the siblings need more professional systems and governance in the enterprise.

Changing Focus

The systems that require most attention change over generations. In generation one, focus is usually placed on the business. Likened to a baby, the business requires nurture and attention to see that it grows to its fullest potential. The dominance of the founder as sole investor and leader of the family enables them to occupy the other two roles very informally and interweave this multiplicity of roles with grace.

In generation two, however, focus needs to switch to the family and the ownership systems. The challenge is that we all tend to make the mistaken assumption that what got us to where we are today will take us to where we want to be tomorrow; this could not be further from the truth.

In James Grubman's book, Strangers in Paradise, Grubman makes an excellent analogy exploring the similarities between the journeys that ethnic immigrants take to a new land, and the economic transformation business families undergo from working-class to affluence, generation one to generation two. He explains that the wealth creators are "Immigrants to Wealth" while their children are "Natives to Wealth." Typically, immigrants (G1) place a lot of emphasis on their history, heritage, and middle-class values, and attribute their present success to their past actions. As a result, they may place disproportionate emphasis on the business when thinking of succession planning. However, just as financial advisors often say past performance is no indicator of future performance, it is important that families understand that they are in a different land now and they must do things differently to succeed.

From Micro to Macro

I love a good window seat when I'm traveling alone by air. I play games with myself, like seeing how long I will be able to track a particular vehicle. I tell myself stories about who the driver is and where they're going, and who the passengers are. What strikes me every single time is that initially I'm able to track this vehicle, but suddenly it fades away into irrelevance as the speed of the aircraft accelerates. I'm soon blown away by the beauty of the macro, as the city or rural landscape is captivating, forgetting the detail of the micro.

As families transition to generation two, they also need to appreciate the beauty of the macro landscape: focusing on a strategic helicopter view of the entire enterprise, rather than focusing on minute details of operations of any given business. The ability to see key trends affecting the macro is critical, as now the family is juggling multiple businesses and wealth. As they soar to greater heights, they must perfect the art of strategy rather than operations. Staying deep in the detail at operator level will drag them down such that they don't see the bigger picture and make decisions in a silo.

Leading family business advisor John Davis explains that families need to evolve from having an operator's mindset (where focus is on operations of the business) to an owner's mindset. Davis explains that thinking like an owner entails excelling at four types of strategic decision-making:

1) Investments: knowing what to invest in, how to manage existing investments, and what to divest of
2) People: knowing how to pick people for critical roles in the enterprise
3) Governance for the enterprise: family, business, family office, and/or foundation
4) Cultivation of the family and enterprise culture.

The owner's mindset is particularly important as families transition to generation two, as typically the enterprise may now consist of more than one operating business, as well as investments. Families need to gain a strategic view of the wider picture, as opposed to get dragged into the details.

Generational transitions are very dynamic, with several moving parts that need to be managed delicately. In embracing the transition, the founder needs to transition from a boss to a mentor, the next generation needs to move from me-focused to we-focused, and lastly the family needs to transition from being conscious operators of the business to being conscious owners. Managing these three transitions in tandem is key to seeing the family business move from lifetime to legacy. They require the family to be connected: enjoying clarity, communication, and collaboration.

CHAPTER 10

Difficult Conversations

A nother common challenge families face when seeking to make a generational transition is difficulty in having hard conversations. The process of succession planning ultimately requires the acknowledgement of several elephants in the room, including money and death. The process requires full clarity on a web of interacting intricate issues. The idea of addressing these can cause anxiety and fear among family members who may prefer to avoid than address.

Money and Death

Unfortunately, we have been socialized to view money as a taboo subject and as such it is seen as impolite to broach the topic. As a result, many founders struggle to open up to their children about it. They may also fear that exposing their children to the full extent of the family's wealth would be a disincentive for them to be productive, independent, contributing workers.

Equally, the rising generation often has many questions on the family's wealth, but do not feel permitted to start a conversation.

This is compounded by the fact that wealth shaming is endemic in our societies. Leading family business consultant David Bork describes how, "In one culture after another, those without wealth seem to harbour a hostile envy toward those with wealth." As such, individual family members may have complex attitudes and identities toward wealth, particularly the rising generation, who may feel like they don't deserve it, as they didn't earn it.

In my consulting work, I often come across next gens who question whether they legitimately earned or contributed toward the family wealth. While typically they may not have full clarity on the extent of the family wealth, their family names command societal recognition as people of wealth due to their parents' reputation in the marketplace. As such, they frequently feel a dissociation, as though it is not theirs. Many feel that it is a stain on their person—an impediment to authentic personal and romantic relationships. This is worsened by a feeling of being eclipsed by others projecting on to them a sense of entitlement, and consequently feeling imprisoned by their circumstance. With such heavy negative emotions toward money, it can be difficult for them to address the topic, and so a culture of silence pervades, while anxiety and fear of the future brews.

In addition to difficulties in having conversations about money, often families struggle to have conversations about death. In the family enterprise, oftentimes family members have a deep fear of the founder's death.

The founder is typically central to the leadership of the family and the business. They would typically have built the business from scratch, and built a founder-centric business where they dominate decision-making. They would typically be surrounded by helpers as opposed to co-builders. Many family members then have deep anxiety about the viability of the business and thus their financial security once the inevitable happens. Founders often share this fear of their own deaths: typically, being type-A personalities, founders are often worried that they will not achieve all their plans in their lifetimes, so often hesitate to let go, and shame themselves into silence.

We Africans particularly have an aversion to facing the reality of death. We are socialized not to contemplate death, and it is considered a taboo to think of or discuss. This is because according to the traditional African belief system, life is cyclical, not linear—the dead are believed to be alive in a different realm.

I remember when I first began my consulting practice, I was very desensitized to this delicate topic, given my British exposure as well as my upbringing. In my family, we would have very open conversations about death, and I thought that was normal. It may have been normal to me, but it certainly was not the norm! In conversations with potential clients, I would talk about death quite crudely, lacking sensitivity; one founder said to me, "Why are you always talking about my death? Are you trying to wish it upon me!"

This fear of bringing upon death by discussing it is not unique to us Africans and/or to founders alone, it is a common fear around the world. As a result, many business families find discussion of succession traumatic and prefer to avoid than address.

Suppressing Emotions

The succession planning process therefore requires addressing heavy emotions, namely fear, anxiety, and shame; however, many families find it difficult to do so. We live in a largely patriarchal society with strong stereotypical male and female behaviors. For example, men are expected to be detached heroes while women are expected to be nurturers. In addition, our cultural beliefs about emotions are often gendered. For example, media portrayals of cancer patients depict women as needing to use emotion management skills to battle their emotionality, while men's battles are depicted as a test of their character.[24]

As a result of patriarchy, many of us have been conditioned to consider stereotypical female behaviors as "less than" and unimportant compared to stereotypical male behaviors. Consequently, families subconsciously tend not to prioritize addressing emotions, and instead suppress them.

Suppression of emotions is not often a successful strategy. Like snowflakes can accumulate over time and cause avalanches, suppressing emotions can lead to loss of control and incomprehensible damage. Despite this reality, families find it easier to discuss ancillary issues rather than root issues. For example, it is easier to have an argument about differing opinions of strategy to pursue in the business and/or wealth than it is to address the fear of the founder passing away, the shame the founder feels, or any other longstanding issue in the family. Families tend to have surface-deep conversations, like doctors treating patients' symptoms without doing thorough examinations to understand and treat the root causes.

The Art of Holding Difficult Conversations

The irony is that just when families need to hone the skill of holding difficult conversations, that's when they typically clam up and create this culture of silence. The generational transition from one to two is particularly delicate; it is considered to be a high risk one with regards to the fate of the family and enterprise. In Nigeria alone, it is estimated that over 98% of family businesses fail to outlive their founders.[25]

This statistic paints a grim picture, but is still not the full picture, as it fails to capture the negative impact on the family. Oftentimes, families are ravaged and torn apart irreparably by conflict during such seasons. Moving from generation one to two is likened to crossing the sea; where the quality of the bridge used to cross is compromised, the transition is at stake. To build a quality bridge, families need to invest in holding difficult conversations during the lifetime of the founder.

This is such a critical period because the family is undergoing a change in dispensation, from founder-led in generation one to a siblings partnership in generation two. It is likened to the family evolving from a dictatorship to a democracy.

I remember growing up in Nigeria when we were under military rule. Nigeria gained her independence from the British in 1960 and led a relatively successful democracy for just six years. She was led by military rule from 1969 until 1999. Thereafter, she transitioned to a democratic rule.

The difference under both dispensations was like night and day. Under military rule, the military governors and heads of states ruled by decree. There was no need to consult citizens in governance, and there was little accountability. As a result of this top-down hierarchical governance culture, whereby military leaders led at a distance, citizens had little ownership of the nation. They largely complied and most didn't question. There was little collaboration and dialogue between government and citizens in seeing the development of the nation. People had legal citizenship but not emotional citizenship.

Flash forward a few decades to 1999, when Nigeria transitioned to a democracy. It was completely different: we citizens finally had a voice at the polls by electing officials to serve us. Not only did we have a voice at the polls, we also had dialogues through civic engagement. The result of this was greater collaboration between government and citizens in the development of the nation, greater diversity of thought, and a greater sense of freedom among citizens who could now contribute their ideas. There was a greater level of emotional citizenship, a sense of having skin in the game and a sense of pride toward the nation.

Generation one businesses are like dictatorships. The founder is typically a strong central figure in decision-making in both the family and the enterprise, and in setting the culture (i.e. values, vision, and mission), which they have often set informally. The founder has often used their discretion to decide on contentious topics such as remunerating family members who work in the business; entry criteria for family members in the business; and mode and method of inheritance for family members. The founder has often served as the de facto CEO, board of directors, leader of the family, and shareholder and enjoyed a lot of power and influence.

Finding a Constructive Voice

Many decisions made by the founder go unquestioned by family members and employees, even when the stakeholders do not agree with the founder. This is because quite often various stakeholders do not feel they have sufficient emotional ownership in the business to have a voice. Note that there is a distinction between legal and emotional ownership. The former refers to the legal rights to possession, by way of owning shares or being a beneficial owner; the latter refers to a sense of connection, belonging, identity, permission, and autonomy.

As family businesses in generation one tend to have strong founder-centricity, their voice typically reverberates strongly throughout the family enterprise as in an echo chamber, while other stakeholders nod in compliance. This is particularly worsened in honor cultures,[26] where elder dominance is prevalent, as well as in cultures where positional leadership is prevalent.

In Cross Cultures: How Global Families Negotiate Change Across Generations, by Dennis T. Jaffe PhD and James Grubman PhD, leading family wealth advisors describe the honor cultures that are a diverse ethnic cluster consisting of the Middle East, Latin America, Southern Europe, India, and Africa. These cultures are characterized by the fact that "Emphasis on reputation and social respect and honor and position is strongly influenced by the hierarchies one inhabits." As such, this phenomenon of the echo chamber tends to be worse in such cultures.

When the founder passes away, this central leadership figure is gone. Governing is forced to evolve from a dictator style to a collaborative democratic style. Family members feel licensed to find their voices, but oftentimes they use their voices to protest rather than project. They may have conflict over issues and may fail to collaborate in decision-making, which leads to a break-down in the democracy and consequently failure to move the family enterprise forward. It is at this point we see the benefits of a "dictatorship," where a central leader is able to quickly influence the nation and achieve cohesion.

It is important in this transition from dictatorship to democracy that focus goes beyond just the creation of legal governance structures; there must also be a commitment to strong political leadership, a system for accountability, and a process for civic engagement. Through civic engagement, citizens enjoy a platform through which they can project their voices on matters and issues that may be divisive in the nation (such as tribal, community, and social issues, and schools of thoughts on the economy). The participation of these citizens in the political process influences policy making, and so improves the quality of the democratic governance.

Similarly, for families to have quality collaborative partnerships, there must be a forum where members can project their voices on contentious matters: these matters may include family branch politics, the role of in-laws, the role of extended family, and/or the role of women. Family members must go beyond protesting alone, they must project their voices in a constructive manner, not a destructive manner. By doing so, they move from being reactive to being proactive; they are able to shape culture, rather than react to it.

The art of holding difficult conversations during the

lifetime of the founder is key to this generational transition: the family benefits not only from increased representation but also from greater influence of stakeholders. However, for families to hold difficult conversations, they must first be well connected.

CHAPTER 11

The Secret Sauce – Family Resources

When I was a teenager, my mom would encourage me to join her in the kitchen to learn how to cook. Saturday mornings were when she cooked for the week. My bedroom was right above the kitchen, so I would often be awakened by Mom singing very loudly. That was my cue to join her—I would jump out of bed, get in the shower, and hop to it.

We would usually make stews, jollof rice, and other Nigerian soups to keep us going for the week. We would prepare the ingredients, she would explain the process, and I would assist her. I often observed that she wasn't scientific in her approach—it was all quite intuitive and very subjective. She closely guided me: "A pinch of this, a dash of that, when the soup is not watery again you turn down the fire a little bit ..." I would laugh and ask her why she just did not prepare a recipe that had precise measurements and timings. She would tell me that this was how her mother taught her and this was our tradition.

At age 18, I went to university and was no longer sous-chef. I was now the head chef, in between many a take-out and canteen food. Every now and then, I would try to replicate the dishes I had made under Mom's tutelage. Clearly, I had become rusty because while my cooking was great, the food just did not taste the same as Mom's amazing cooking! I did not take down any notes and had forgotten certain details. It dawned on me that Mom had a "secret sauce" to her cooking. Without carefully documenting her recipes, I ran the risk of not being able to replicate them.

A similar phenomenon is present in our family enterprises. The multigenerational financial success of the enterprise is likened to the delicious aroma of a great meal. In order to generate this aroma, we must use the right recipe. However, we are often unaware of both the vastness of the ingredients used and the appropriate mixes to generate their secret sauce: it is this secret sauce that gives off the alluring aroma. Without careful reflection and documentation of these recipes, we are likely to forget the recipes and unable to pass them on to the next generation. The legacy families should focus on passing on is the recipe, not just the aroma.

The Family Ingredients

Families are often unaware of the ingredients used in their recipes. These ingredients include family capital and family values. Families often overemphasise the importance of their financial capital, unaware of the plethora of capital they have deployed toward the generation of financial success.

In Dennis Jaffe's Six Dimensions of Wealth: Leaving the Fullest Value of Your Wealth to Your Heirs, he outlines six sources of family capital:

- ❧ Spiritual capital: the family's shared mission, vision, values, and purpose of their wealth
- ❧ Financial capital: assets, income from businesses, and/ or investments
- ❧ Human capital: the skills, competence, and character of family members to manage the wealth
- ❧ Family capital: the ability of the family to stay connected and work positively and productively with one another
- ❧ Structural capital: the governance structures required to manage the family wealth including constitutions, councils, committees, and boards
- ❧ Societal capital: using social networks and relationships

It is the combination of the different types of capital that generates financial success, not just financial capital. In fact, many experts argue that social capital is the most important one. According to Dr. Willy Bolander, an assistant professor of marketing at Florida State University, and Dr. Cinthia Satornino, assistant professor of marketing at Northeastern University, up to 33% of the variance in sales performance can be attributed to a founder's social capital.[27]

Bolander and Satornino's findings are key in highlighting the way non-financial capital plays a key role in financial success of businesses, but while their study highlights the importance of the founder's social capital, it understates the importance of other family members' contribution of capital in a family enterprise context, since their study was focused on entrepreneurs.

In a family enterprise context, not only is the founder depositing a range of capital into the enterprise, but the enterprise is also receiving capital from a range of family members. Thus, the multigenerational success goes beyond the founder alone. To optimize success, it's important to not only be aware of the range of capital available, but also the relevant mixes of capital to create the secret sauce. In order to do so, we must collectively reflect and be well connected.

Changing the Capital Mix

This collective reflection is particularly important as we transition beyond generation one, where decision-making evolves from being founder-led to being under a collaborative siblings partnership. The changes may necessitate a change in the family's capital mix and/or in the family's capital contributors. To speak metaphorically, these changes may necessitate a change in the family recipe, as the family members' taste evolves.

For example, consider a manufacturing business based in Rwanda that has been run by the founder, Joseph, who is the father of three children. To generate financial success, the founder leveraged financial capital (investments into the business), human capital (his leadership capacity), and societal capital (his networks and reputation in Rwanda). The founder has been working with an investment banker locally and decides to sell the business when he retires. His three children are based in the U.K. and show no interest in leading the family business.

Instead, he will set up a family office in London using the proceeds of the sale of the business. The children will be beneficiaries of the family office.

Two of the children work in financial services, and one works in a non-profit. They have developed great global networks through friends from boarding school and university, and through joining family office associations. They plan to leverage their network by identifying appropriate investment opportunities for the family. In addition, they have identified a governance consultant to assist with establishing a decision-making process for the family office. This consultant has facilitated family meetings so that the family can collectively deliberate on what their purpose, mission, and vision is with respect to their wealth. Lastly, one of the children intends to join the family office as an executive team member.

The family's capital mix has changed: structural capital, spiritual capital, societal capital, and human capital are more prominent than ever before. The family spends more time considering their purpose, leveraging their network to find suitable investment opportunities, and developing a family constitution for the family office. Not only has the capital mix changed, but the capital contributors have also changed. The success of the enterprise moves from being concentrated on just the founder's sources of capital to also including the rising generation's sources of capital, as they contribute more than ever before. The connectivity of the family is a necessity in allowing for this elasticity in capital mix and capital contributors over time.

The multigenerational success of a family business is like a by-product. It is important to master the art and science of creating the main product, particularly as your family seeks to make a generational transition. It's important to look back and reverse engineer the process by which the main product was made in the past. In addition, it is important to look forward, and anticipate needs for product upgrades and innovation, such that there are tweaks to be made to the process. By focusing on the process and not the goal, you set yourself up for greater success.

CHAPTER 12

The Role of Family Dynamics

One of my favorite pastimes is to binge-watch Netflix shows—yes, I'm one of those, and proudly so! I pride myself in finding shows from different parts of the world with unique storylines. A couple of years ago, I stumbled across a Spanish series and got hooked: Unauthorized Living was a gem; there were 100 episodes and each one was 82 minutes long—very bingeworthy!

Unauthorized Living is similar to Succession (which I also highly recommend!). It's about the owner of a family business, Nemo Bandeira, who wants to retire. However, he is diagnosed with Alzheimer's disease and decides to keep his condition from his family, while deciding on who among his children will be the successor of the business. All the while, Open Sea, the family business, is about to go public.

As if that wasn't enough drama, the writer throws in some additional bonus plot twists. Firstly, the business is not actually into shipping—that's a cover-up: it's heavily involved in drug smuggling. Then we learn Nemo had a secret adult child, Lara, who had been estranged from the family. She tries to integrate into the family as an adult woefully. This creates jealousy on the part of the other two children. The other children, Nina and Carlos, also have sufficient drama in their lives: Nina is a social-ite dating Nemo's lawyer, and Carlos is a horse breeder who is in and out of rehab with a drug addiction.

There's a lot going on in the show, and it is a perfect case study on family dynamics. Despite the family drama, we see a high level of interrelatedness demonstrated between the family members. Like a chain of dominos, actions taken by one family member impact another member, which impacts on another member. Eventually, the whole family unit is affected by the actions of one person, whether consciously or unconsciously!

The study of dynamics is a branch of physics concerned with the motion of objects. Dynamics are about patterns and processes that yield movement, change, or transformation. In a family, the study of dynamics looks at how its inner workings impact the family's movement. These inner workings are commonly its communications, hierarchies, roles, and patterns, while its movement is its ability to transform. They can either propel or inhibit the transformation.

Al Ubaidi defines family dynamics as:

> The scheme of family members' relations and interactions including many prerequisite elements (family arrangements, hierarchies, rules, and patterns of family interactions). Each family is unique in its characteristics; having several helpful and unhelpful dynamics. Family dynamics will ultimately influence the way young people view themselves/others and the

*world. It will also impact their relationships/behaviors
and their future wellbeing."[28]*

The study of kinetics in physics is a subtopic of the study
of dynamics. This subtopic looks specifically at how dynamics
are influenced by force, mass, momentum, and energy. Similarly,
family dynamics are also influenced by a range of factors, both
internal and external.

Internal factors include the nature of the parents' relationship, the number of children in the family, the personalities
of family members, significant events that may have affected
family members (such as divorce, affair, trauma, death, financial difficulty, and family violence), and family values. External
factors include influence from extended family, and social,
economic, and political external systems. Family dynamics are
therefore impacted by anything and everything!

There are factors that can have a positive impact on family
dynamics, and factors that can have a negative impact on
family dynamics. Just as in the study of kinetics, not all forces
bring about motion: friction, for instance, resists motion. Forces
therefore can be constructive (i.e. induce movement), neutral, or
destructive (i.e. inhibit movement). Similarly, in families, dynamics can be constructive (help connectivity), neutral, or destructive (inhibit connectivity).

Constructive dynamics promote positive behavior and help
ensure that every family member receives emotional support,
whereas destructive dynamics threaten the emotional support and behavior within the unit. However, the presence of
destructive forces does not mean gloom, just as the presence
of friction does not necessarily mean no movement. Families

can intentionally counter destructive forces to move in the right direction. It is possible for them to be subjected to negative forces, yet be better connected. The beauty is that every family is unique.

In No Man is an Island, the English poet John Donne famously wrote, "No man is an island entire of itself; every man is a piece of the continent, a part of the main." Donne alludes to the interdependence of the existence of humans, as we are not wholly independent, and the fact that we are a collective humanity.

Such interdependence is commonly observed in families, and is explained by Bowen's family systems theory. The theory was developed in the late 1940s by Murray Bowen, a U.S. psychiatrist. He spent his life studying individual and family behavior. His theory departed from previous ones that saw the family as one emotional unit, and the individuals as part of that unit; rather, he saw the family as an autonomous psychological entity. One of the implications of this theory is that family members are affected by each other: changes in the behavior of one family member will impact how the entire family functions.

Culture and Dynamics

Not only are men not islands, but arguably families are also not islands: they are reflections of their cultures. Mahatma Gandhi said, "A nation's culture resides in the hearts and in the soul of its people." Therefore, it is impossible to divorce cultural norms from family dynamics.

In collectivist cultures (commonly found in the Middle East, Latin America, Africa, and Asia) where there is greater emphasis on the community than the individual, the extended family tends to play a more prominent role than in individualist cultures. Grandparents, aunts, uncles, and cousins are an intimate part of the family network. In addition, there tends to be a prevalence of "non-family family," i.e. relatives who are unrelated by blood but considered family members.

Furthermore, non-monogamous marriages can impact on family dynamics, namely polygamy and polyandry. Polygamy is where marriages involve husbands with more than one wife and polyandry is where marriages involve wives with more than one husband. Polygamy is more commonly observed than polyandry. Though polygamy is not commonly practiced in the West, it is legally and widely practiced in 850 societies globally.[29] It is highly common in West Africa: in Senegal, 47% of marriages include multiple women.[30]

This adds a level of complexity to the family dynamics: research demonstrates that there tends to be a higher incidence of marital conflict and disruptions in polygamous marriages.[31] In addition, there tend to be strong hierarchies of wives, based on order in West African polygamous marriages. Marital satisfaction tends to also be significantly impacted by wife-order, where happiness tends to be highest among young only wives, followed by older only wives, then young subsequent wives and lastly older subsequent wives.[32] This gives an insight into the fact that there may be significant heterogeneity among wives and their children in a polygamous household.

The highly integrated extended family, the concept of non-family family, and the non-monogamy commonly observed in collectivist cultures can have a significant effect on the family dynamics, because there are more players contributing to and reacting to the family dynamics. Although this complicates the family dynamic, it does not automatically lead to unhealthy family dynamics. Families are like writers who hold the pen, subconsciously or consciously determining the nature of the dynamic.

How Family Dynamics Impact the Business

Unauthorized Living also demonstrated that not only do family dynamics impact the entire unit, they also impact the business. Episodes unveiled how ongoing relationships in the family would impact decision-making in Open Sea. For example, Nemo had a loyal longstanding lawyer, Mario, who was vying for the successor role. However, Mario started having a secret relationship with Nina, to Nemo's displeasure! The show demonstrated that the family and business were not independent—rather they were interdependent. The Bandeira family is not unique in this regard, as this typically holds across all family businesses.

Family businesses consist of family and business systems that often have conflicting objectives: the family system seeks to provide a nurturing unit for members, and is like an emotional bank, whereas the business system seeks to make a profit, and generate a return on investment, like a traditional bank. This interdependence can lead to family dynamics impacting the business.

Dalai Lama said, "Just as ripples spread out when a single pebble is dropped into water, the actions of individuals can have far-reaching effects." The dynamics within a family can also be like a pebble that creates ripples. These ripples have far-reaching effects beyond the family unit—they can impact the business.

For instance, a commonly observed family dynamic impacting the business is the extension of a parent-child relationship into the business sphere, whereby the child is kept in an infantile role—always a little one in the parent's eyes. This can result in the parent questioning the child's decisions, questioning their competence, and being condescending. Instead of being treated as a colleague or partner, the successor is treated as a child. Consequently, the successor may feel resentful, and the ripple effect of this family dynamic can have disastrous effects: not only can it strain the parent-child relationship, but it can also create friction among other relatives. Sometimes, such friction can be so combative and bitter that it leads to the demise of the business.

Moving Toward Healthy Dynamics

For families to move toward healthy dynamic, they must choose to enforce boundaries. In her book, In The Company of Family, Melissa Mitchell-Blitch explains that boundaries teach families "Wisdom to know how to balance family relationships, individual well-being, and business vitality—some of the key priorities which often compete at the intersection of family, business and wealth." Families can be healthy where there is a delicate balance of independent individual family members and an interdependent family unit, or unhealthy, depending on the choices the family makes: unhealthy family dynamics are not automatic.

Commonly observed unhealthy family dynamics include enmeshment, where family members are too connected and lack independence; triangulation, which is when a third party is drawn into conflict between two family members; and recurring conflict.

Family dynamics have implications not only across space (impacting the family unit), but also over time. The family unit often inherits dynamics from previous generations. Like a snowball that accumulates snowflakes, families accumulate dynamics over generations. Their pasts influence their present. The impact of dynamics reverberates across time.

Trauma and Family Dynamics

The implication of this is that at any given point in time, families may be impacted by significant traumatic events of their pasts. These may be events that have long passed, but have left an indelible mark. Trauma is deeply subjective: it is simply a response to what an individual finds to be distressing or disturbing. There are no objective criteria to evaluate which events will cause trauma. As such, it can be precipitated by war, financial difficulty, exposure to addiction, terminal illness, etc. Trauma is individually experienced, yet this subjective feeling can impact one's lineage for generations to come. Recent research shows that through epigenetics, trauma can reverberate through generations.[33]

The challenge is that family members are often unaware that they have inherited said trauma. This is because it is individually experienced and often causes people to clam up and to suffer secretly in shame. Yet, like an asteroid that has hit the family unit, it leaves a mark. The consequence is that while each family member is born into someone else's story, they may be unaware of it because often in families there are missing conversations between generations: missing conversations of pain, regret, fear, and shame that each member would rather suppress than share, even though sharing usually leads to healing. Consequently, they pass this trauma on to the next generation and to the next and the next. There are lessons to be learned from said trauma, but until family members start having conversations to acknowledge and address these issues, the cycle will continue.

Consider a family with a history of alcoholism. Perhaps a late great-grandfather was an alcoholic, and this pattern was passed down in the family. Even though the great-grandfather has passed, the family has inherited a pattern of alcoholism and strained relationships as a result of his lifestyle. Great-Grandfather perhaps concealed, lied, and avoided, and these behavioral patterns were modeled to other family members. Thus, this late family member continues to influence present family dynamics.

How Dynamics Change

Another implication of this is that family dynamics are likely to change in the future. Families that are undergoing generational transitions may soon encounter pivotal events such as retirement, illness, or death of a parent that can dramatically disrupt dynamics. Parents often occupy a central figure in the family, leading the unit and ensuring that members communicate with one another. These pivotal events can dramatically disrupt patterns of communication, family relationships, and dynamics among the siblings.

Further, as families progress into generation two, siblings experience changing dynamics individually, as they navigate increased prominence in the enterprise and collectively, as they form a partnership. Lastly, the focus of the siblings moves from the nuclear to the extended family: siblings may get married and have children of their own. Siblings are now navigating whether their loyalties lie with their family of origin or their newly founded family. In addition, the extended family grows to now include in-laws and grandchildren.

Navigating these dynamics so that they are constructive and not destructive is critical for business families crossing the generational gap. This requires an awareness that can only come about in families that are well connected.

Independence and Interdependence

On July 4, 1776, the United States Declaration of Independence was pronounced in Philadelphia, Pennsylvania. In the declaration, the 13 American colonies severed their political connections with Britain, declaring their independence. The historic event culminated in the formation of the United States of America as we know it today: the leader of the free world, a nation that champions liberty, self-government, equality, and individualism.

Today, centuries later, the quest for individual independence has spread beyond the borders of the U.S. to the rest of the world, due to the "Americanisation" of global culture. The consequence of this is that independence is a common aspiration that many have been conditioned to seek: our societies, education systems, and media promote independence rather than interdependence.

Independence means one is not reliant on other people to survive and exist. In families, independent individuals pursue their purposes, passions, and visions with no support or interaction with other family members. Often, the hallmark of success is when a teenager becomes an "independent" adult, able to stand on their own feet financially and emotionally, outside of their parents and siblings.

In contrast, interdependence refers to a mutual reliance on other family members in pursuit of purposes, passions, and visions. This dependence can be on physical, emotional, and financial resources. There's a shift of focus from the individual alone to the collective family unit. Interdependence is not unidirectional—it is mutual.

The independence-interdependence concept is not binary; rather, it is a spectrum: nations cannot enjoy absolute independence or absolute interdependence. For example, for the United States to be absolutely independent, they would have to operate a closed economy, with zero engagement in international trade. In reality, no nation is absolutely closed, as they need to import raw materials/goods/services produced elsewhere to function.

Similarly, the U.S. is not absolutely interdependent with other nations: this would require a complete dependency on other countries for the nation to function. The closest governance structure to such interdependency is exemplified by colonies. A colony is a territory subject to rule by its colonizers. Though dependent on their colonial masters for political, economic, and social governance, colonies still enjoy separate administration in their home countries. Complete interdependence can threaten a nation's sovereignty.

Interdependence and Independence in Families

By the same token, absolute independence and interdependence are both impossible and ineffective in families. Family members are dependent to some extent on each other for their physical, emotional, and financial needs: no baby comes into the world able to fend for itself. Equally, family members enjoy some level of independence as no one else can tend to their physical needs like eating, sleeping, and exercising.

Families can therefore choose an appropriate blend of independence and interdependence. In choosing this, it is important that the pursuit of independence of individual family members cannot be to the detriment of the interdependence of the collective unit.

Ken Ginsburg puts it this way:

> *Gaining independence is a central developmental challenge of adolescence. If we think of our children as young birds reliant on us for their survival, we can view teens as having to learn to spread their wings to ultimately fly from the nest. However, we don't want to be left with an empty nest. We want our children to be "in flight"—comfortable as they soar on their own and confident as they choose to return to the nest for landings. We honor and foster independence on the road towards interdependence."*

In the same way, family enterprises should strive to honor and foster independence on the road toward interdependence. The data also supports the thinking that interdependence is critical in generating multigenerational success, as highlighted in Dennis Jaffe's study of 100-year families. His study evaluated 100 families across the world that created, sustained, and/or expanded wealth for over 100 years. Jaffe called these families "generative families." He observed that there were strong commonalities among these generative families. One of the observations was that while these families had individual performers, they had a shared commitment to working together. In essence, they had strong interdependence.

Interdependence is mutual, meaning that all family members are dependent on one another, and all contribute their polycapital toward the collective; it is not co-dependence, where members cannot function outside of each other, nor is it dominance. Interdependence does not require uniformity of perspectives, preferences, and priorities, but it does require unity, where family members have a clear understanding of their shared purpose, vision, and mission. The shared identity may differ from the individual family members' identities. Lastly, interdependence is achieved through inspiration and not legislation, meaning family members do not feel a sense of obligation but a sense of willingness.

The Importance of Interdependence

Interdependence is so important for business families because as families of wealth are transitioning across generations, their wealth becomes more complex in ownership, as the number of owners typically increases. Families need to learn how to navigate shared ownership and shared decision-making.

They must foster the skill not just of independence but also of interdependence.

Interdependence as a goal is important in a family enterprise, as it is often a critical ingredient in its secret sauce. Over time, the family may have forgotten this ingredient, and the sauce loses its taste. In the early days of the business, the family may have been highly interdependent: family members were asked to make sacrifices of their time and money to keep the business going. The family may have gone through challenging financial seasons together. During these tough times, they build up a bond, like soldiers at war who develop camaraderie, nurtured through the hardships of the battle.

After some time, the business hit an inflection point and moved into a growth phase where revenues, cash, and profits grew rapidly. In the good times there was no obvious need to pool the human and financial resources of the family. The bond was not actively nurtured. Instead, as the family's financial wealth grew, the founder may have actively encouraged the independence of the children, rather than their interdependence.

In addition, the founder may have placed emphasis on the management of just the financial wealth. As a result, as the family transitions into generation two, the family may look to split the financial wealth, so each family branch manages theirs independently. This scenario is commonplace in business families.

The truth is that interdependence generates greater impact than independence: pooling capital as a family would yield greater financial returns as a result of economies of scale. There's something magical about scale. Impact does not grow in a linear fashion, it grows exponentially. Just as one puts a thousand to flight and two puts ten thousand to flight, a collective of independent smaller-scale family branch investing will not have the transformative potential of pooled larger-scale family capital. Families can pool capital to enjoy greater returns as well as shape the world in a transformative, sustainable way through social entrepreneurship and impact investing.

Interdependence is also a source of competitive advantage when it comes to management of a family business. Through collective leadership, the business is able to benefit from diversity of thought and collective wisdom, knowledge, and intelligence of contributors, generating synergies and greater quality and quantity of solutions. On the other hand, businesses that lack interdependence are usually led by individual rulership, putting them at a disadvantage, as they lack variety in vantage points, and limit their pool of ideas.

In addition, the connection represents more than a strengthened familial relationship. The connection also leads to an accumulation of family wealth, made up not just of financial capital, but also of spiritual, human, family, structural, and societal capital, or "polycapital." The capital is deposited by all the family members. This allows for the family enterprise to be able to tap into greater sources of capital during disruptive times so that they can forge forward together.

As well, camaraderie is not an ancillary benefit of interdependence, but rather is the core raison d'etre for the family members. Like soldiers in battle, family members develop a strong bond that sustains them. As Douglas R. Satterfield said, "Men fight in war not to achieve a strategic aim but because of their comrades fighting alongside them. Camaraderie is their motivation." Just as camaraderie is the motivation for soldiers, connection serves as a motivation for business families. The loss of this camaraderie has significant effects and can be a hindrance to the multigenerational success of the enterprise, as it represents the loss of a common focal purpose for the family.

It is important to note that there are situations in which interdependence is not viable: one must make room for nuance and complexity. For instance, there may be strained relationships in the family, or there may be a lack of alignment in purpose, vision, and mission that may necessitate that the family members go their separate ways, choosing independence over interdependence. While it is important to make room for nuance and complexity, it is also important that families are conscious of the importance of interdependence, and are not seeking independence on autopilot, blindly sacrificing the potential gains of the collective. Instead, they should weigh their particular situation and choose the appropriate blend of interdependence and independence that suits them.

Management of family dynamics is critical for business families, as oftentimes destructive family dynamics can lead to the demise of the family enterprise. It is key to navigate these dynamics such that they are constructive, so that families can maximize their interdependence, bringing about stronger relationships, a greater pool of capital, and diversity of thought.

CHAPTER 13

Africa Overview

A couple of years ago, I was on Arise TV, being interviewed on generational wealth on the African continent. It was a live interview, and I was so nervous about messing it all up. My stomach was turning, my hands were trembling, and I was trying to compose myself so that my voice didn't shake. I prayed that the host would take it easy on me with the questions.

The first question was simple: "Why have we not seen much generational wealth in Africa?" I set the scene, explaining how, unfortunately, the continent has lagged behind her global peers in terms of transferring and stewarding generational wealth and businesses, and that there lies an opportunity to learn from our global counterparts that have been more successful at doing so. I was just getting into the groove of it and hadn't yet died from the experience when the host decided to turn the tables on me completely unexpectedly!

Just two minutes in, he asked whether I was advocating us eroding our culture to adopt and copy the established norms, practices, and protocol of our global counterparts. How did we get from A to Z? I thought. This made me even more nervous. I'm sure my blood pressure had risen significantly by this point, as I looked at him with a "Whatchoo talkin' 'bout, Willis?" look!

The gentleman assumed that I was a victim of cultural imperialism, ready to subscribe to all things Western, even if it means that we lose who we are in the process. Far from it! I explained that I am proudly African. The uniqueness of Africa is the beauty of Africa. I do not believe in imitating. As Samuel Johnson said, "Almost all absurdity of conduct arises from the imitation of those we cannot resemble."

I explained that what I do believe is that instead of imitating, we should be aware of our cultural nuances so that we can empower ourselves to define practices that suit our situation. We do this by observing others' journeys and adapting to our situations accordingly. In the process, we give ourselves agency to shape our futures.

An outcome of this careful reflection is that not only will we be able to import solutions adopted by our global counterparts that can serve us, but we will also be able to export widely established African practices that can serve the world. The conversation can shift from one of assumed cultural imperialism to export of knowledge, i.e. what African family businesses can teach the rest of the world.

But before we jump to saving the world, let's take a step back to understand the specific nuances we face as family business owners on the African continent. Africa is the second largest continent in both size and population, and boasts a diverse cultural heritage. It's important to appreciate that she as a continent is very distinct across regions in her history, culture, economy, business environment, and family structure.

The Uniqueness of Our History

I came across a quote by Robert Heinlein that really struck me. He said, "A generation which ignores history has no past and no future." Powerful words. The reality is that often on the African continent we do ignore our history. For many, this ignoring is unconscious, as the education system has robbed them the opportunity. For example, during the 2009/2010 academic session, history was removed from primary and secondary school curriculums in Nigeria, robbing a generation of the gift of historical context: events such as the Nigerian Civil War that occurred so recently in history (between 1967–1970) are not being taught. This is tantamount to censorship and dilution of our true stories.

When we do not understand our history, we are unable to build our futures, as our history is our collective story, and our stories and narratives give us identity. In addition, our history gives us clues as to why we are where we are and the way we are. It provides lessons that we can learn from, so that we can forge a stronger future.

First things first—disclaimer: I am not a historian. I am just an avid reader and curious about narratives. I will attempt to share some of my learnings on our inherited narratives.

So what is unique about our history? Africa is said to be the birthplace of humanity and boasted of kingdoms and empires across the continent, including the Kingdom of Kush, the Land of Punt, Carthage, the Kingdom of Aksum, the Mali Empire, the Songhai Empire, and the Great Zimbabwe. The oldest of these kingdoms, and one of the most prolific, was the Egyptian Empire, which reigned between the sixteenth century BC and the eleventh century BC.

These kingdoms often had great control over resources and external societal affairs through councils. In addition, they often co-existed peacefully, collaborating significantly with outside kingdoms and tribes: there were major trading routes across the continent where goods were able to be traded with those outside of the continent. The significance of trade of items such as gold and salt gave rise to the development of major trading cities such as Timbuktu, Gao, Marrakech, Tunis, and Cairo.

A dear friend and colleague of mine, Tsitsi Mutendi, says that we often look to the West as having the first family offices globally; however, these African empires can be considered the true first family enterprises globally. They were great models for governance, succession, inter-regional cooperation, and trade.

In addition, communalism was commonplace. African communalism was characterized by groups of people with common values, beliefs, and interests living together, sharing and organizing themselves collectively in community. The collective was more important than the individual. Individuals were identified and known through their communities. Assets such as land were commonly owned, whereas others such as cattle could be owned individually.

Social philosophies such as "Ubuntu," which means, "A person is a person because of others," were prevalent on the continent. Ubuntu essentially speaks to the fact that we are a collective humanity, and this spirit was ingrained in the social fiber. The community always came first.

As a result, one sought to honor the dignity of others and was concerned with the development of mutually affirming relationships. Ubuntu expresses compassion, reciprocity, dignity, harmony, and humanity in the interests of building and maintaining community with justice and mutual caring.

The introduction of religion, namely Islam and Christianity, had a significant impact on our societies. Islam came first in first century AD, followed by Christianity. Prior to that, traditional religions were widely practiced, and a lot of these traditional religions were not monotheistic but polytheistic, believing in multiple gods. Polygamy was widely practiced across the continent. Christianity introduced the idea of monogamy, which was counter-cultural, whereas Islam allowed for polygamy.

Islam and Christianity relied heavily on their religious texts for spiritual authority, while traditional religions had no written texts; instead, they derived authority from oral history and practices. Flash forward to today, one sees a confluence of traditional and organized religious influences, whereby many Africans fuse traditional and Muslim or Christian practices. In addition, one sees a situation where polygamy is still widely practiced even among Christians.

I've always been fascinated by the idea that there are corridors of power and rooms where the world's most powerful meet and make many decisions that affect you and me. These meetings do not necessarily come with a fanfare, a red carpet, and press coverage, but in them, the most influential decision-makers gather behind closed doors. These folks may not be many in number, but they make a tremendous impact. One of such rooms was in Berlin in 1884–1885 during the Berlin Conference, where European leaders convened and decided they were going to go on a "Scramble for Africa." The French, Brits, Belgians, Germans, Portuguese, Italians, and Spanish all made their land-grabs and the continent was divided among the European powers: by 1914, 90% of the continent was under European control. This meeting in Berlin, though attended by a few, shaped the trajectory of billions of people on the continent, affecting even you and me today. It was the birthing room of colonialism in Africa.

Colonialism stripped colonies of their political power. It altered governing and legal systems. It laid a foundation for economic exploitation: colonies were merely economic interests to their colonizers, seeking to maximize their returns. For centuries, this backdrop of economic pursuit contributed to the transatlantic slave trade. Lastly, it shaped culture.

Pre-colonialism, Africa was a continent that practiced heterarchy, meaning equitable gender relations: while men and women may have had different roles, they had similar status in communities. As the continent was so large and sparsely populated, a huge premium was placed on the ability to control labor. This meant that motherhood was respected and so were women. They were also respected for their roles in communities as grandmothers, business owners, and religious leaders.

Gender equity was a feature of many Bantu tribes. In fact, in the approximately 500 Bantu languages spoken in Sub-Saharan Africa, terms such as "woman" and "man" are not frequently used even today; for example, in my language, Yoruba, there are no gender-specific words for son, daughter, brother, sister, etc.

Historians such as Diop argue that African systems were actually matriarchal, with inheritance and succession passing through the female line. For example, Pharaonic Egypt and the West African Sahel empires were matrilineal. This meant that power and status were maintained as women married.

A huge disruption to gender relations was the transatlantic slave trade and colonialism. The idea of misogyny and patriarchy was imposed by the colonial powers, who followed a different world view: they tended to believe in the superiority of men, and this was enshrined in social, political, economic, and legal practices.

Not only did colonialism have a significant impact on the continent, it also had a non-uniform influence on Africa. For example, the French promoted an ideology of assimilation in her colonies, pushing for an adoption of all things French culture, whereas the British were less aggressive in that regard. Until today, France has significant influence over her former colonies, through currency management, tax payments, and military agreements. Significant diversity can be seen across the continent today as a result of the different approaches these two major colonial masters took. In addition, there were a couple of countries that were not colonized, namely Ethiopia and Liberia. This aspect of their history has uniquely shaped them.

Flash forward to today, and we see a continent that boasts of rich cultural diversity, heritage, and influences: a large continent with over 1.3 billion people, 3,000 ethnic groups, and 2,000 languages, far from its monolithic image. In fact, we have a continent full of cultural complexity, and it is important to be culturally intelligent to understand the themes that influence the continent.

Despite the significant cultural heterogeneity, some common values are shared across the continent.

Communality

In Africa, "The individual is like a community-culture bearer".[34] The sense of importance that is placed on the collective is shared across the continent. This is rooted in our history, where assets were communally owned, profits were communally shared, and relationships were also communal.

It is no surprise that our sense of community has persisted until today. We see huge levels of giving, both formally and informally, and this has influenced family business owners. We have wealthy individuals who have established formal foundations such as Aliko Dangote's Dangote Foundation, Nicky Oppenheimer's Brenthurst Foundation, Strive Masiyiwa's Higher Life Foundation, and Mohammed Dewji's Mo Dewji Foundation.

However, as with most things in Africa, looking at the formal sector would lead to a great underestimation of the true picture: Africans give on a daily basis, mostly informally, of their money and time to support those less fortunate. There's a consciousness ingrained in the hearts of most, to support those at risk of being left behind. For example, the unemployed, the orphaned, the start-up entrepreneur, the elderly, and the widowed.

This communal, high level of interdependence and cooperation is also modeled in financial management: Esusu is a term used to describe traditional forms of financial cooperation in Africa where groups of people informally contribute to savings and credit for their mutual benefit. This practice was started by Yorubas in Nigeria, and spread across West Africa. The spirit behind this cooperation is that the welfare of the collective community is more important than that of the individual. They understand that as the entire collective gains, the individuals gain.

A Sense of Kinship

Linked to our communal thinking is a strong sense of kinship. Kinship refers to sharing of characteristics or origins. In Africa, associations based on ethnicity, clan, religious affiliations, and/or common interests can be as strong or even stronger than blood associations. There's a fluidity in the concept of family, such that non-blood relations can be considered as family.

One of my dearest friends and co-laborer in this field of family business is Tsitsi Mutendi. Tsitsi and I are co-founders of a non-profit organization called African Family Firms. I consider her a sister, as we've built mutual trust and respect for one another. We have common values, outlook, and vision for ourselves as individuals and also for our community.

Tsitsi and I will commonly refer to one another as "sister" to third parties and on social media, as we have the sort of commitment to one another that blood relations share. An associate of ours actually thought we were blood sisters! He was shocked when he found out that we were not in fact sisters connected by blood, but sisters connected by heart.

This connectivity with heart is commonplace across the continent, whereby a business owner may have left their village for the city and become successful in the city, but their heart remains in their village. They continue to support their community of origin through knowledge transfers, cash donations, infrastructure projects, etc., ensuring that their kin are supported and developed. Some go as far as placing their kin on the company payroll, to ensure that their needs are met.

Reverence of Elders

Across the continent, elders are to be accorded huge amounts of respect. Elder figures typically occupy positions of authority and their decisions are to be unquestioned. This feature of a centralized authority can be observed in our history in the ancient Yoruba kingdoms, the ancient Benin kingdom, the ancient Ashanti kingdom, and others across the rest of the continent. There were definitely no appeal processes, and what the authority said was final!

William Conton said, "Africans generally have deep and ingrained respect for old age, and even when we can find nothing to admire in an old man, we will not easily forget that his grey hairs have earned him the right to courtesy and politeness."

As a result, elders are deeply respected: they are deemed wise, and their wisdom is to be both honored and unquestioned. The challenge in placing such a huge emphasis on the wisdom of the elders is the stifling of the youngers. It can be deemed disrespectful for the young to criticize or challenge authority figures in positions of leadership in family, government, and society at large, family businesses notwithstanding. As a result, the younger may stay silent, not because they approve of the status quo, but because the dominating culture may choke their voices, leaving them apathetic and disengaged.

The average age of African political leaders is 62, older than the OECD median, while the average age of her citizens is 18, among the youngest in the world. The irony—the youngest continent on the globe has the oldest rulers in government. While these statistics reflect leadership in politics and government, they also paint a picture whereby next gens not only face a crisis of underrepresentation in politics and governance, but also often in family businesses. This disengagement has real costs and limits the potential of the business as oftentimes next gens are "More knowledgeable, equipped, and prepared to address the fast moving issues of today than the establishment leadership."[35]

Non-uniformity of Gender Relations

My last theme is a bit of a copout as it refers to the non-uniformity of gender relations on the continent; far from a unifier! I often say that there's a lot of lazy anthropology that paints a single story of gender in Africa, and that story is often dominated by an oppressed, helpless, marginalized group.

In 2021, writer Chimamanda Adichie wrote an essay entitled, "It Is Obscene." In it, she passionately criticized the "cancel culture" that is prevalent in today's discourse, particularly among younger generations on social media. She wrote about the importance of educating oneself such that one can intelligently defend one's ideological positions. She said that many seek to "Flatten all nuance, and wish away complexity."

I wholeheartedly agree: flattening all nuance and wishing away complexity can disempower an entire generation. The truth is that there is no single story on the topic of gender. Yes, gender discrimination exists and is a real issue to be dismantled: in our arena of family business, female-founded businesses tend to be outperformed by their male counterparts. In addition, there remains a prevailing culture of primogeniture whereby the oldest son will succeed the founder.

However, a single story does not allow for nuance and

complexity. For instance, according to the BBC, Nigeria has the highest rate of female entrepreneurship globally, with over 40% of women being business owners. Thus, it is important to appreciate nuance and complexity. This nuance and complexity arises from the fact that Africa is vast: Nigeria alone, just one of her 54 countries, has over 370 ethnic groups and 500 languages,[36] and each ethnic group has its subsets of customs, practices, and norms.

History challenges this single story of an oppressed gender: as explained previously, historians such as Diop and Professor Ifi Amadiume have shown that African systems were actually matriarchal. For example, in the Yoruba tribe, chieftancy titles such as Iyalode and Iyaoloja were reserved for women. Iyalode was "an intermediary between the leading male chiefs and the town's women"; it was the highest-ranking female chieftaincy.[37] The "erelu" was a place reserved for females on the king's council of elders. Similarly, in Nnobi, an Igbo community in Eastern Nigeria, the political system was matriarchal: the Ekwe women were the leaders of the marketplaces and the Women's Council was a political organization of all women in the region, which excluded men.

History also suggests that women dominated trade and the marketplace throughout Yorubaland. They played a key role in trade and could acquire wealth. The chieftaincy title Iyaoloja was reserved for women and was a role for the head of the marketplace.

In Gender and Female Power in Yorubaland, Sarah Jenise Mathews explains that the two Yoruba concepts of female power, the deity Aje and the concept of aje, establish "the culturally ingrained importance of female power." She further explains

— 138 —

that the deity Aje was a goddess of the marketplace. Aje represented wealth, trade, and money.

These two concepts tell us two things: one is the importance of womanhood and female power in Yoruba culture and the second is the importance and dominance of women in the marketplace. Throughout history, women have run the marketplace and most of the trade in Yorubaland.[38]

Women were strong in their communities: often at the helm of the grassroots movements, they had strong voices politically. An example is the Igbo Women's War in 1929 where thousands of women challenged British colonialists. The women accused the colonialists of trying to limit their roles in government through the introduction of "Warrant Chiefs," which they deemed unfair. In response, they organized themselves and led a protest. Consequently, in 1930, the British abolished the Warrant Chiefs.

The dominating conversation on gender is one of raising consciousness about the patriarchy. However, this conversation is void of discussion of the matriarchy. Instead of a binary situation, what exists today is a spectrum of patriarchy/matriarchy as a result of colonial and religious influences. Some tribes today are still matrilineal, for example, the Akan people located in Ghana and Ivory Coast.

The implications of this spectrum of patriarchy/matriarchy means that there is significant variation in terms of gender empowerment on the continent. This depends on the tribe of the family, their religion, their individual values, whether they are rural or urban, etc. and these influences can shape views on gender.

While we may have a long way to go in terms of gender equality, it would be folly not to acknowledge the positives: there is a raised consciousness of the role of women, and we have fierce women founders and successors who are paving the way for the uprising generation and modeling possibility.

Having done a whistle tour through history of the continent, and unpacked the common values and themes we see on the continent, in the next chapter I'll proceed to highlight the relative advantages we have as a community in building generational businesses, and potential areas for improvement.

CHAPTER 14

Our Natural Advantages

n the last chapter, we unpacked cultural anthropology, to explain why Africans are the way we are. Now we will proceed to unpack why we are poised for generational success.

This may seem counterintuitive to you as you read: what natural advantages could we possibly have when we lack a track record of high levels of intergenerational wealth? It's counterintuitive, but hang with me.

Consider this scenario: David is 6'2" and is 12 years old. He is the tallest among his peers. People repeatedly suggest to him that he should play basketball. He joins the basketball team and is the tallest in the team. The trouble is that David does not attend training regularly. Also, he is not regimented about his exercise and nutrition. While David has a natural advantage, he has not perfected his skill by engaging in process, and as such he is not optimizing his potential.

Many African families are like David. Through no fault of their own, they have not engaged in the right processes to ensure they are on track toward legacy wealth. The awareness of the nuances of family businesses and the necessary building blocks to ensure we move from lifetime to legacy are at a nascent stage. As such, like David, many of our families may have a natural advantage, but are not optimizing their potential.

Back to my initial statement, then—why are we poised for succession?

Our Resiliency

Let's be real, "Africa is an extreme sport!" as often said by my sister/co-partner, Tsitsi Mutendi. We have embodied volatility: volatile political and economic environments, wars, dictatorships, and relatively weak institutions. Over the past century, the continent has undergone massive transformations, moving from colonies of European powers, to gaining independence, to seeing several civil wars and coups. The irony is that this volatility may be a source of strength, as we adapted and infused resilience in our family businesses.

COVID-19 has been bad. However, many family businesses across the continent had faced prior disruptions and become accustomed to them. From seeing huge devaluations of currencies, to experiencing civil wars and coups, to dynamic business conditions, these businesses had embodied adaptability—otherwise they would not have survived.

Data would seem to support this thinking: leading family business researchers Devin Deciantis, M.P.P. and Ivan Lansberg, Ph.D. conducted a study[39] on family businesses in emerging market environments, which corroborated this sentiment. They found that "Family-controlled firms that survive frequent existential threats have built resilience into their organizational DNA" through strategic planning. They found that families in these environments had also created a network that "Provides a reliable and diverse source of funding, deal-making and government relations in the absence of mature markets for capital, information and political representation." This social capital was a critical competitive advantage.

In my humble opinion, social capital is the most important type of capital a business family needs. Growing up, my father always emphasized what he termed as our critical success factors come values: 4Hs and 2Ps: Hard Work, Honesty, Humility, Harmony, People, and Places. He always told me and my siblings that these were all we needed to go places in life. So, it's been ingrained in me to focus on building social capital through seeking, nurturing, and cultivating relationships with people from a range of places. I was not taught to focus on amassing financial capital, as my father would often stress that social capital typically leads to financial capital.

Families often have a rich social network and can draw upon this capital to maximize their existing businesses or set up new businesses. As such, this social capital often leads to financial capital. Founders can also pass on their social capital to the next generation, who can build upon it as a platform to soar.

Natural Governance

As I explained earlier, we are a very communal people. As a result, there is a consciousness of our interdependence in major decision-making affecting all aspects of our lives.

A great example of this is getting married: in most African cultures, marriage is not between two individuals, it is in fact between two families. From the get-go, the entire community is involved in the union. Most tribes have a formal process for suitors to go through when they want to get married. The suitor must be vetted by the elders, and there are customs and rites to be undertaken before the couple is accepted as a conditional unit!

All these demonstrate family governance. Governance is a word that typically comes with dread! I mean, who likes the word governance? Not only does it come with dread, but it also can be quite intimidating.

About a decade ago, I started my legacy journey. As a second-generation business owner, I was keen to see that the family enterprise that my parents had built up would stand the test of time. I began researching, learning, and connecting. I would consistently hear of "family governance," but the word governance would put me off. It seemed archaic, irrelevant, and quite frankly a distraction to running the business.

Governance conjured up an image in my mind's eye of an old bookshelf with lots of dust on it. Above this bookshelf was an outdated grandfather clock. And on the bookshelf were lots of documents that contained a lot of formality, pushed aside because in reality no one ever looked at these documents nor cared about them.

What I associated governance with was a whole bunch of outdated rules and structures that no one really cared about: councils, charters, and committees that were bureaucratic, burdensome, and boring.

It was later that I realized that governance is just a means to an end. It is an enforcer to the "this is how we do things around here." It is a facilitator to managing relationships, to communicating effectively, to allowing for participation and engagement, and for decision-making. In essence, at the heart of governance is connection and conversation. These are all great, and critical to the smooth running of a family and a family business!

I also had clarity that the spirit of governance is more important than the letter, i.e. what it enabled was more important than its legal forms. Just because my family did not have councils, committees, and charters did not mean we did not have governance, as the absence of formality is not the absence of governance!

Ken McCracken, leading family business expert, termed "natural governance," where family members know what to do without "deliberate human design." He debunks the myth that "A family enterprise that lacks formal structures, such as a board of directors or a family council, is a void in which governance does not exist."

Many of our nuclear and extended families practice natural governance unknowingly: we know which aunt to call to mediate conflict, or which cousin to contact to organize family events. Or which uncle to contact to provide counsel on training and development. Or how to escalate issues. We just need to extend this sphere of influence of natural governance to include our family enterprises.

Bridge Across Generations: Reverence of the Elders

Another contributor to our natural advantage is our reverence of elders. In Africa, we honor those who are older, as they are deemed wiser. We demonstrate this honor by giving them titles: Sir, Lady, Chief, Elder, Pa, Ma, etc. Calling an elder by their first name is deemed disrespectful. In addition, we typically consult them for their wisdom. This is critical, as we are able to draw from their wisdom, knowledge, and intelligence, allowing a transfer from the older generation to the younger generations.

This is particularly important as family businesses undergo generational transition, when the founder of the business is seeking to pass the reins to the younger generation. The founder can ascend from boss to mentor, where they can pass on their knowledge and expertise to the younger generations. They can leave a legacy of entrepreneurship through doing so.

In his book, Family: The Compact Among Generations, Jay Hughes explains the roles that elders typically play in family enterprises:

- Mediator: Resolving and mediating disputes in the family to maintain family unity and trust
- Advisor: Advising the family when it is not following the "rules" adopted by the family
- Storyteller: Telling stories to the family to remind them of their legacy
- Rituals: Maintaining and implementing rituals and ceremonies in the family.

These four roles are critical in ensuring a smooth generational transition.

Storytelling

When I was a young child, my parents would often have my aunts and uncles in the house. Imagine six, seven, eight Yoruba adults gisting over food and drink; of course it was vibrant! Instead of playing with my cousins and siblings, I would often sneak away and sit at the bottom of the stairs and eavesdrop on their conversations.

The gist was always sweet! They could be speaking about how paint was drying on a heritage building, but they would say it in such a way that was engaging and captivated my attention. They would use voice and gestures to bring their tales to life—that was more interesting to me than playing Red Rover.

Africans are natural storytellers. Storytelling is in our DNA; it is in our history. In many parts of the continent, after dinner, villagers would come together around a fire to listen to stories.[40] So storytelling was a communal experience. The stories told would often have moral lessons infused into them, and often parables would be told.

I often tease my mom about her inclination to weave in proverbs and parables. We could be talking about going to school or church, and somehow an ancient Yoruba tale or proverb about a lizard finds its way into our conversation!

African stories often share a certain style and structure. They are not just reciting or reading facts; they infuse metaphors, voice, gestures, and rhythm, and they are vibrant. It is through storytelling that we preserve our history, customs, and culture.

In West Africa, griots (male) and griottes (female) are oral historians and storytellers. They are the social memory of communities, and keepers of facts. They have the responsibility of passing down knowledge from generations to generations. They have knowledge of ancestry and genealogy and are called upon at important events to recall a family's history through song.

The benefits of this storytelling are enormous. Stories are one of the most persuasive forms of communication: tell people a fact, they may remember, but tell people a story, not only are they unlikely to forget it, but they are also often inspired. Stories allow for transfer of knowledge and information to the younger generations. This art of storytelling can be applied in the family enterprise to foster greater connectivity within the family.

So, what can we do better?

Building on Resiliency

Our resiliency is laudable, but a danger of being exposed to constant volatility is that one is inclined to become focused on surviving and not thriving. This inclination is subtle and often subconscious, and one becomes short-term oriented as opposed to long-term oriented. Ultimately, one embraces a lifetime mindset as opposed to a legacy mindset.

It's like the fable about a frog being slowly burned alive. The frog is put in a pot of lukewarm water which is being slowly heated. Unaware of the danger looming, the frog stays in the pot, and is eventually boiled to death. Dramatic corollary, I know! But I reckon that it is powerful and relevant imagery. What is boiling our family enterprises to death is often our mindsets, as a lot of us are unconscious of how our volatile environments have impacted them.

Sitting on the edge of your seat, conscious of the fact that change may happen at any point—for instance, the government can change policy drastically overnight or the currency can lose value overnight—can make you focused on the immediate here and now that you can see and be assured of, as opposed to longer-term strategic planning, as there are so many unknowns.

The trouble is while there are many future unknowns, we must plan today for tomorrow, so that we are not naked tomorrow. Through diversification, risk management, and institutionalizing, we can protect ourselves to ensure long-term thriving. It is key that we have an awakening, such that, in spite of the environment, we consciously seek to embrace legacy. The irony is that if we fail to embrace a legacy mindset, our next generation may be exposed to the very poverty that we are trying to avoid currently.

Another implication of this volatility is often quick decision-making, and what I term U-turn decision-making, i.e. we made a strategic decision today to enter a new market, and tomorrow we go back on that decision because of new realities. This volatile, impromptu decision-making is necessary to survive. The challenge is it can be difficult in such scenarios to institutionalize the learnings, the wisdom, and the intelligence that the founder imparts to the next generation.

It is thus key that we focus on being intentional about being legacy-oriented, such that we institutionalize knowledge, wisdom, and intelligence so the next generation can forge forward.

Formal Governance

While natural governance is a legitimate form of governance, it leaves room for lots of ambiguity. In order to provide clarity, at some point families should consider formal governance. This is especially true for us Africans as our families are more complex in size and in composition than our global counterparts. For instance, polygamous homes, non-family family, and more disruptive business and political environments call for one less unknown in our business families.

Family governance is similar to the governance of nations. As families move from generation to generation, they become larger and more complex. Natural governance becomes more difficult to implement. Just as nations require formal governance to avoid anarchy, families also require formal governance to bring sanity, clarity, and transparency. These are brought about through constitutions, councils, and committees.

We can seek to build upon our natural inclination toward governance by seeking to formalize the foundation of connection and conversation.

Giving Room to the Rising Generation

While reverence of the elder is important, one of its unintended consequences is the stifling and silencing of the younger. Young people are to be seen and not heard. The expectation is that they are to be told what to do and are not to contribute. This can lead to the rising generation lacking emotional ownership, feeling that they are not valued and feeling that they do not belong. A risk is that they will become apathetic and disengaged in the family enterprise. The issue is that they are lacking intrinsic motivation.

Motivation speaks to why we do the things we do. This can come from outside (extrinsic), for example, one may be driven by status, monetary rewards, or avoiding punishment. Or it can come from inside (intrinsic), where one engages in something because they find it rewarding on the inside. Intrinsic motivation is a more effective long-term method to achieve goals, as extrinsic motivation can lead to burnout over a long period of time.

On my podcast, I had a conversation with Sharath Jeevan, a leading global expert on motivation, about his work and its application to family businesses. In his extensive research on inner drive, he found that there are three critical tenets required: purpose, autonomy, and mastery. This means that for the rising generation to be intrinsically motivated about the family business, they must have a sense of purpose, knowing how the family enterprise helps and serves others; feel a sense of autonomy, believing in their individual ability and agency to change things for the better; and mastery, being on a continual journey of self-improvement.

The challenge is that this stifling of the younger generation limits their autonomy: many feel voiceless and powerless, unable to effect change in the family and family enterprise, and as such lack inner drive. The consequence of which is that we do not see as much collaboration between the generations. This limited collaboration does not allow for reverse mentorship, i.e. the transfer of wisdom, intelligence, and knowledge from the younger generation to the older generation. For instance, the younger generation are more technologically inclined and may hold the clues and keys to how to navigate our 21st century digital world. In addition, the median age in Africa is 18, and 84% of the population are millennials or younger. Such, the younger generation are more in tune with the pulse of the consumer.

We should seek to build bridges across the generation, allowing for two-way knowledge exchange, enabling both traditional and reverse mentoring.

Non-oral Stories

Our inclination toward oral story-telling is like a double-edged sword: on one hand, it's extremely persuasive as a tool of communication and acts like a glue, creating cohesion within families and communities. On the other, it can lead to limited impact, particularly when we look from a generational perspective. Many of us are now urban African business owners, having left our villages of origin. In migrating, we left behind many traditions such as the griots and griottes, who passed on our histories from generation to generation orally. Yet we are yet to imbibe a culture of being intentional about passing down our stories non-orally.

My paternal grandmother passed away in early 2021, and it was a difficult loss for me to process. She had been frail for about a decade, and so I had anticipated her transition. However, the reality of her loss was quite different: my heart felt it in a way that my head did not. It was painful to think someone who was critical in raising me was no longer. Her death took me back 13 years prior, when my grandfather, her husband, passed away. Memories of me with them flooded my head and my heart, and I felt deep sadness that they would be no more.

I also felt deep anger and a sense of violation that I had been robbed of my ancestry and heritage. I had regrets about not taking enough time to ask my grandparents about their stories and their origins. I had a deep longing to know my ancestry, to trace my genealogy, to understand my identity, but there was nowhere to turn. There were only limited written documents and pictures of them when they were younger.

In my search for a connection to my heritage, I came across a letter my grandfather wrote to me when I was just eight days old. I was born in London, and my grandmother was around for my birth, but my grandfather unfortunately could not make it. He was on a work trip in Spain, and so missed both my birth and naming ceremony. As head of the family, he would have anchored and hosted my naming ceremony. In his absence, he sent a letter. It was simple and brief, saying:

> *My dear baby, your name shall be Modupe Olanike in the name of the Father, the Son and the Holy Spirit l'oruko Jesu Amin (in Jesus' name Amen).*
>
> *Love, Your Grandaddy,*
> *Chief S.O. Olowolafe*

Finding this letter brought tears to my eyes. Tears of joy: I felt connected to Granddaddy once again. Seeing his handwriting brought back so many memories. I could also hear his voice, imagining him reading out the words he had written. I felt a reconnection to my ancestry and heritage, a heritage in which grandparents played a key role in not only the naming but also the rearing of a child. Yet I wished that they had shared more letters throughout their lives, chronicling their journeys, and sharing their values and vision for the family. I wished that they had recorded these not only in letters, but also in video form and audio.

The chronicling of stories in non-oral forms is a powerful tool for fostering intergenerational connections and is equally applicable in business families. Families can seek to write letters, capture videos, audio, and photos to convey the origin story and the evolution of the business and the family and their wishes for the future.

It's important that we work to harness our natural advantages such that we build stronger family businesses that outlast, successfully moving from generation to generation. In doing so, this rewrites the economic story of our families, ensuring that we are not exposed to the plague that is poverty, but rather have engines of generational wealth. In addition, beyond the impact on our families, the continued legacy of our businesses provides much-needed jobs, alleviating poverty. Collectively, this rewrites the nation's and continent's economic story.

In summary, we can solidify these natural advantages by being intentional about building connected families that have clarity of mission, vision, and values; communicate well within and across generations; and collaborate. The 3Cs. I unpack how to build the 3Cs in the next three chapters.

CHAPTER 15

Clarity of Vision, Mission, and Values

"Cat: Where are you going?
Alice: Which way should I go?
Cat: That depends on where you are going.
Alice: I don't know.
Cat: Then it doesn't matter which way you go."

— *Lewis Carroll*

lice in Wonderland was one of my favorite stories as a child. I didn't realize at the time that there were some heavy life lessons woven into a seemingly light children's book, one of which is the importance of clarity. Just as Alice needs clarity about where she is heading in order to know which way she must go, families also need clarity in where they are going to know which way to go.

Players in a sports team also need clarity of vision, mission, and values to succeed. Players need to know what success looks like; the vision, strategies, and tactics they will employ to be successful; the mission; and which team they are on. The same holds for business families. Families need to have a shared vision, or where they are going, a shared mission, or the direction they are taking, and shared values, or the essence of who they are. In absence of this clarity, families are unlikely to succeed.

COVID-19 was a huge lesson on disruption: families started a new decade with plans that were suddenly made irrelevant. They were forced to learn to work in new ways, and reinvent their platforms, products, services, and perspectives. Collective clarity of vision, mission, and values can help families turn this complexity into opportunity: moments of disruption provide a great opportunity for reimagination, reinvention, and renegotiation.

Shared Clarity

In the first generation, the vision, mission, and values may be locked in the head and heart of the founder. However, transitioning to the second generation, the family needs to be intentional about explicit definition that is agreed upon by all members. Otherwise, in absence of this explicit definition, there is likely to be conflict among family members as the family transitions to the second generation. This is because these may be imposed by one dominant individual, or the family is unable to gain consensus on their shared vision, mission, and values. This conflict can threaten the survival of the family enterprise.

Lack of clarity also leads to collective brain fog. Brain fog is a feeling of confusion and disorganization where one finds it difficult to focus and/or articulate one's thoughts. Those who have brain fog describe having "fuzzy thinking," or "cloudy thoughts." This lack of clarity can lead to decision paralysis as families are overwhelmed with endless decisions to make in their enterprises.

Yet the disruptive hour our business world is in calls for decisiveness. The storm of COVID-19 and our 21st century industrial revolution has led to declining revenues, profits, and cash flows for many family enterprises. Consequently, there's a need to identify new opportunities that are viable in this changed world. The challenge is that families face a fast-moving world where a year is like a month and a month is like a week! This fast-moving world means fast-changing viable opportunities. Ironically, the abundance of opportunities to consider creates decision inertia.

The Cost of Decision Inertia

The phrase "paradox of choice" was coined by psychologist Barry Schwartz. He found that increased choice leads to greater anxiety, indecision, paralysis, and dissatisfaction, as those tasked with making many decisions have greater fear of making the wrong decision. The pressure is on: a lot is at stake. The greater the stakes, the harder it becomes to make a decision. Science indicates that harder decisions wear out our brains, and our executive functions become less effective.[41] Consequently, families can feel confused and drained, and thus avoid making decisions.

The challenge is that this decision paralysis has a cost: "More is lost by indecision than wrong decision. Indecision is the thief of opportunity. It will steal you blind," as Marcus Tullius Cicero said. Families must take quick decisions with conviction to ensure their enterprises are back on course, especially in these highly disruptive times.

A 2017 study[42] of leaders found that "High-performing CEOs do not necessarily stand out for making great decisions all the time; rather, they stand out for being more decisive. They make decisions earlier, faster, and with greater conviction." Being decisive is more important than being right.

Clarity acts as an enabler, to allow families to take quick decisions with conviction. This is because by knowing where they intend to go, they are able to eliminate countless potential destinations and accompanying routes. They are able to use their shared vision, mission, and values as a compass to guide decision-making. They are able to eliminate distractions. Clarity therefore gives business families a cutting edge; it makes them nimble, agile, and adaptable, key advantages in our modern world.

Families therefore need to be clear on their shared vision, shared mission, and shared values.

Shared Vision

Vision is where the family intends the enterprise to be; what the family wants to see in the future or in the long term. Just as one needs clarity on a destination when one is embarking on a journey, a family needs clarity of vision when working together. Getting clear on this shared vision is a critical success factor and predictor of effective integration of the next generation.[43]

Peter Senge says, "When people truly share a vision they are connected, bound together by a common aspiration. Personal visions derive their power from an individual's deep caring for the vision."

Therefore, it is important that the shared vision is derived from individual members' personal visions: they can see their personal visions in the collective vision, such that it is clear how enlisting in the collective family vision achieves their personal vision.

Shared Mission

If a vision refers to a destination, the mission refers to the route taken to get to the destination; it is how the family will actualize the vision. A shared mission therefore incorporates all the family members looking at the high-level initiatives to be taken by the family members to achieve the family's goals. If the vision is a "what," the mission is a "how," i.e. what the family intends on doing in the next one to five years to move toward the vision.

A shared mission fosters a sense of ownership, as each of the family members is part of the mission, not just the implementation. A shared mission incorporates the missions of each of the family members.

Shared Values

Values refer to the essence of a person, the principles or standards of behavior that one deems important. Values are the core identity of a person and reflect one's heart and soul. Shared family values are the values that family members commonly deem as important, and these shared values are also reflective of the family's heart and soul.

As I was growing up, my father would always repeat our values. He summarized them as the 4Hs and 2Ps: Humility, Honesty, Hard Work, Harmony, People, and Places. Though these values were simple, they were profound. They served as a glue in our nuclear family, as we had a commonality and a bond. Quite often, such family values impact the enterprise's values, given the high interdependence frequently observed between the family unit and business unit.

As Daniel Geltrude, managing partner of Geltrude and Company, says, "In many of the family businesses we work with, including the extremely wealthy ones, values play a very important role in the strategies of the firms and how important decisions are made. They're the principles upon which these affluent, successful families run their lives and their companies."

Values are therefore a key ingredient in the family's secret sauce. The family needs to reflect and consciously define these values.

It is frequently said that "values are caught, not taught," but I believe that this saying is unhelpful in a family setting, as the onus is on the entire family to collectively define and agree upon its shared values. To say values are caught not taught implies that there is a location that they are caught from; it also implies that it is a passive process. Instead, families have agency to decide which values they would like to pass on to future generations.

Just as players of a sports team need clarity of vision, mission, and values to succeed, business families also need clarity of shared vision, clarity of shared mission, and clarity of shared purpose to succeed. Families must be intentional and not passive about seeking this clarity, as it helps with eliminating options and facilitates better decision-making.

CHAPTER 16

Collaboration and Leadership

A few years ago, I was at home with our two sons and overheard a conversation between them. Ire, the older, was four at the time, and Ayo was 18 months and just learning to talk. Ire and Ayo's personalities have always been like day and night—Ire is very prim and proper and likes things by the book, whilst Ayo is extremely free-spirited and jovial, and he loves to wind up his big brother!

Ayo had just started daycare and was obsessed with saying, "A, A, apple" and, "No no no no." I was upstairs and the boys were at the top of the stairs. I overheard Ire shouting at Ayo, saying, "Come downstairs now!" Ayo responded "No no no no" and then proceeded to point at the stairs saying his classic "A, A, apple." This left Ire super frustrated, and he went off and threw a tantrum because his brother refused to go downstairs with him!

That incident taught me about leadership: leadership is about collaboration and not domination. Had Ire explained what was in it for Ayo to go down the stairs, I am so sure he would have followed! Or had Ire been open to Ayo contributing his idea on where they should go, perhaps there would have been more success.

Effective Leadership

The word leader comes from an Old English word meaning "to go before as a guide." Leaders are to guide not dominate, to facilitate not dictate. Contrary to popular belief, business families do not have one leader (the founder/CEO of the business). In fact, all family members are leaders. They go before as guides of their enterprises, collectively casting a vision, formulating a mission, impacting businesses, investments, and communities. To do so effectively, family members must collaborate.

Leadership requires effective use of power. Martin Luther King defined power as "The ability to achieve purpose and effect change." Families are striving to achieve purpose and effect change but they must deploy this power appropriately. Ire was demonstrating power over, as Brené Brown says, asserting his supposed power over his younger brother, as opposed to demonstrating power with, seeking to share power with him. Power with builds on a foundation of connection and empathy, and everyone wins! As families transition beyond generation one, they also need to share power among family members, through cultivating a culture of collaboration: it's about collective leadership, not individual rulership.

Families are like sports teams: team members must collaborate effectively with one another to win the game. This becomes more urgent as a generational transition is imminent: in Nigeria only 2% of family businesses survive beyond generation one, compared to 33% globally. [44]

To see an increase in this 2% statistic, families need to cultivate a culture of collaboration vertically, i.e. across the first and second generations, and horizontally, i.e. among the second-generation siblings. These siblings will have to learn to work together effectively; therefore, it is critical that they perfect the skill of collaboration to build legacy enterprises.

Effective Collaboration

Collaboration is not a walk in the park! Vertical collaborations can be challenging due to a commonly observed wide divergence in perspectives between generation one and generation two: founders tend to be more past-focused, i.e. "How have my values, heritage, and history gotten me to where I am today?" whereas next gens tend to be more future-focused, i.e. "How can I change the present to shape my future?"

In addition, horizontal collaborations can also be challenging. Often siblings have never practiced being partners; they have largely deferred to the matriarch or patriarch's decision-making. They have extensive experience as siblings, but little to none as partners. Many become "accidental partners": they do not anticipate being partners, and have to unexpectedly grapple with the huge responsibility of jointly managing family assets, operating businesses, investments, and philanthropy. [45]

Therefore, the challenge of our day is how business families can learn how to collaborate effectively. For the first time in history, we are seeing up to five generations co-existing due to rising life expectancies. Families must learn how to collaborate vertically. Furthermore the "great wealth transfer" will see up to $68 trillion passed on to the next generation by 2030.[46] Many of these inheritors are from family enterprises and will need to learn how to make decisions in conjunction with their siblings. So, families also need to learn how to collaborate horizontally.

In Simon Sinek's book, Leaders Eat Last, he says that the Spartans, a warrior society in ancient Greece, "were feared and revered for their strength, courage and endurance." Their power rested in their shields, and to lose a shield in battle was the single greatest crime a Spartan could commit: "Spartans excuse the warrior who loses his helmet or breastplate in battle but punish the loss of all citizenship rights the man who discards his shield." And the reason was simple. "A warrior carries a helmet and breastplate for his own protection, but his shield for the safety of the whole line."

Family members should seek to be like the Spartans, putting on their shields for the safety of the whole family. This is not without impact, as collaborative teams lead to engaged teams. Evidence suggests that engaged teams perform better: firms with an actively engaged workforce report 2.6 times the growth in earnings per share than counterparts with disengaged employees.[47]

So, what does collaboration look like for business families?

Not hogging the limelight

Players who desire the limelight tend not to make the best decisions for the team. Their individual need to be seen and praised supersedes the collective need to win the game: they tend to overlook and not include other team members who can contribute toward winning the game. Collaborative team players understand that "It is not the team with the best players that win. It's the players with the best team that wins" (John Gordon).

Similarly, families need to take collective decisions as opposed to having one member dominate.

Passing the ball to the best player

In soccer, the objective is to score a goal and win the match. The player who is kicking the ball need not pass the ball to the closest teammate, but instead critically evaluate the skills, competencies, and potential of the team to know which member to pass to.

Similarly, families need to critically evaluate the skills, competencies, strengths, and passions of team members to know what role they should play in the enterprise. They need not be bound by traditions and expectations.

No spectator on the team

Collaboration is about ensuring that every individual member contributes toward the achievement of the collective team's goals. No member is allowed to be a spectator. Active team members are not necessarily seen on the pitch: the coach and bench players are equally as important to the success of the team as those on the field.

In the same way, all family members must contribute toward the family enterprise. Not being active in the business does not diminish the importance of family member's contributions; other activities in the family council, family foundation, family office, or as board members of the family business are just as critical.

Appreciating our differences

Collaboration not only recognizes the individual contributions toward the collective goals, but also appreciates the different strengths and weaknesses each member brings to the table. The soccer team appreciates a team that is diverse in their abilities and does not resent other team members for being different. They appreciate that the diversity of the team is the strength of the team.

Similarly, all family members appreciate the differences in each other, appreciating that the diversity brought about as a result of age, gender, and diversity of perspectives is key to developing the talent pool of the family. We each process information differently, we each are engaged and inspired by different things, we each have our unique gifts. We can appreciate this cognitive diversity rather than focusing on the differences between us.

Collaboration is a key tenet required for business families to successfully transition from lifetime to legacy. To collaborate effectively, individual family members do not hog the limelight; they pass the ball to the best player, appreciate the differences of other team members, and are not spectators.

CHAPTER 17

Communication

Just 30% of family businesses globally survive into the second generation.[48] Therefore 70% of first-generation businesses will fail to transition. Data suggests that communication is a key reason: 60% of this failure rate can be attributed to lack of trust and communication.[49]

Communication is critical for families. Teams that communicate with one another will work together better, forming a stronger overall team.

Vertical and Horizontal Communication

Teams need both strong vertical communication and horizontal communication: in a soccer team, if a coach fails to explain the goals of the season to the team, the performance may be suboptimal. Further, if the team members fail to communicate with one another on the pitch, their performance may also be suboptimal. Winning teams communicate well.

Similarly, family firms require strong vertical communication—between the first and second generation, and strong horizontal communication—among the siblings partners. Unfortunately, the data suggests that many families have weak vertical communication: many family businesses fail because the head of the family can't communicate their wishes to the younger generation.[50]

Furthermore, horizontal communication may need improving: siblings who may not have been used to working together may fail to communicate effectively, as they may have "Different communication styles, decision-making styles and information-processing styles."[51] These differences can give rise to conflict.

The song Message in a Bottle by The Police is about a guy stranded on an island who finds a bottle, puts a message in it, and throws it out to the sea, as an SOS to the world. He hopes someone will get his message to rescue him from loneliness. The song can be interpreted as an analogy for isolated people desiring connection: communicating a message of distress to others may be their only hope.

The message in a bottle is a great visual, highlighting that the objective of communication is to deliver a message. To ensure great connectivity, families need to ensure that their messages are being appropriately delivered.

Telling All One's Heart

Families must therefore master the art of communication: they must learn to not only send and receive messages on the technical, but also on the emotional. Family enterprises can be emotionally charged as members often carry residual emotions from the family unit into the other units. These residual emotions can be positive (trust, loyalty, joy) or negative (disappointment, fear, shame). As a result, they may be sitting on a keg of gunpowder; explosive negative emotions that can be triggered by a significant event.

For example, sibling conflicts are often triggered by the death of "Mom," who is typically known as the "Chief Emotional Officer" in the family unit. Mothers are often nurturers, mediators, and connectors and often allow for the expression of suppressed emotions as well as actively bridging the gap between differences in siblings, thus resolving conflict.

To ensure that such emotions do not obliterate the enterprise and the family, families need to learn to move past surface level communications to deeper emotive communications.

This requires families to be courageous; however, the word courage often has connotations of something greater than it is.

There is a concept of ordinary courage, and Brené Brown explains it, saying, "Heroics is often about putting our life on the line. Ordinary courage is about putting our vulnerability on the line." Heroism differs from ordinary courage. Families simply need to exhibit ordinary courage by being vulnerable with one another in sharing matters of the heart.

Courage is not necessarily about taking quantum leaps, but it is about the heart. The root of the word courage is cor, which means heart in Latin. In one of its earliest forms, courage meant "to speak one's mind by telling all one's heart." Families need not hide their hearts, but instead get vulnerable. This atmosphere of vulnerability builds trust. In Stephen Covey's words, "Without trust we don't truly collaborate, we merely coordinate or, at best, cooperate. It is trust that transforms a group of people into a team." By delivering messages of all their hearts, families move from individual members to interdependent, winning teams.

Spoken and Unspoken Messages

Communication goes beyond the spoken—it also includes the non-spoken. In The Laws of Human Nature, author Robert Green tells a story about Milton Erickson. Erickson was a psychotherapist who, at age 17, was paralyzed with polio, unable to speak or walk. He was unable to leave his home for months. It would seem this time gave Erickson an opportunity to perfect the skill of reading body language. He observed his siblings, parents, and nurses interacting and noticed that often their verbal communications were not in tandem with their body language.

Erickson perfected this skill of reading and interpreting non-verbal communication. Many actually thought he was psychic—he wasn't, he was just highly observant, having honed this skill over a period of time. For example, Erickson was able to tell when a lady was being unfaithful to her husband: he noticed that her legs were tightly held together. He could also tell when his secretary was on her period as the manner in which she was typing changed—she would chump the keys! Lastly, he could guess people's professions by studying their hands, their gait, and the inflections in their voices!

Non-verbal messages are therefore key, as many clues are given away by our bodies. In fact, data from Ray Birdwhistell, who did a study of kinesics, suggests that over 65% of communication is non-verbal. Families must be observant like Erickson, such that they can interpret both spoken and unspoken cues of their family members, observing facial expressions, gestures, body language, tone of voice, and eye gazes. They must take delivery of both spoken and unspoken messages.

Transmitting and Receiving Messages

Prior to getting married, my husband and I did a pre-marital counseling program. Our instructor recommended that we read Gary Chapman's book, The Five Love Languages. In the book, Chapman hypothesizes that we each have a "native" love language that is our preference to receive as well as express love. The love languages are acts of service, gifts, quality time, words of affirmation, and physical touch.

Chapman explains that what tends to happen in relationships is that each partner typically expresses love in their native language, but this language may be foreign to the other partner: it's like an Arab native speaking Arabic to a Portuguese person—they will fail to understand each other!

Chapman's Love Languages is a great reminder that communication is not just about giving; it is also about receiving. Individuals not only transmit communication, but also receive communication. Communication is therefore like a radio wave that is transmitted through an antenna. The radio wave is received by another antenna attached to a radio receiver. To receive the wave, the antenna must be tuned to the right frequency. If the antenna is not on the correct frequency, there will be no sound.

Similarly, all communication involves both sending and

receiving messages. Sending a message that is never received has the same effect as not sending the message at all. Communication therefore involves the receiver being ready to receive: family members need to be tuned in to the same frequency to be able to effectively understand what is being said, both through verbal and non-verbal communication. They must be on the same wavelength.

Effective transmission is also necessary. The sender must try as much as possible to see a congruence between his/her message and the core meaning. Transmitters and receivers essentially share the responsibility in ensuring effective communication.

Just as winning teams communicate well, winning business families also communicate well: data suggests that most family businesses fail to move past their current generation due to communication-related issues. To win, families must ensure that there is both strong vertical and horizontal communication between generations and among sibling teams. They must not only communicate on the technical, but they also communicate on the emotional, by being vulnerable with one another.

CHAPTER 18

Conversations

A Sudanese proverb says, "We desire to bequeath two things to our children. The first one is roots; the other one is wings." By building an entrepreneurial legacy, families are bequeathing both roots and wings to their immediate and future descendants. Roots represent their collective history and wings represent ability to co-create a new future. It is the combination of the roots and wings that allows the family to be resilient. This ability to co-create is critical for your family in this hour, given the disruptive business environment we find ourselves in. The ability to regenerate, renew, and reinvent is critical to building resiliency so that you can future-proof your enterprise.

These roots and wings can only be effectively transmitted in connected families, where members have conversations.

Conversational Intelligence

Dr. Judith Glaser was an organizational anthropologist who believed that the key to success in life and business was becoming a master at what she termed "conversational intelligence." She believed that those who are able to learn effective conversational skills are able to develop greater trust, partnership, and success. In her book, Conversational Intelligence, she highlights the three common types of conversations:

- Transactional, where parties share information
- Persuasive, where parties are trying to convince others about their point of view
- Transformational, where parties co-create solutions.

She explains further that transactional and persuasive conversations trigger the lower, more primitive brain, which is prone to distrust and paranoia. On the other hand, transformational conversations activate higher-level intelligences, yielding trust, empathy, strategic thinking, and good judgment. These promote the release of oxytocin, the hormone behind connection. Science demonstrates that in order for families to become better connected, they must not only focus on having a greater quantity of conversations, they must also focus on having greater quality conversations. Families must move away from having just transactional conversations to also having transformational conversations.

Transactional versus Transformational

Transactional conversations are essential to running our family enterprises: we need to accomplish tasks, delegate, pay bills, hire people, make decisions, etc. These transactions keep the enterprise rolling so that it operates smoothly. Transactional conversations typically have an "ask-tell"[52] dynamic, i.e. the goal is to inform and confirm.

For example, consider two siblings, Nnamdi and Ifeoma, who are working on restructuring ownership of the family's assets. Nnamdi asks Ifeoma about the status of the legal advice. Ifeoma provides Nnamdi with an update.

While transactional conversations are necessary in the management of family enterprises, they do not foster a connection. In order to build meaningful connection, we need to focus on transformational conversations.

Conversation is defined as the oral exchange of sentiments, observations, opinions, or ideas. Transactional conversation is simply the exchange of information, whereas transformational conversation usually entails a deeper exchange of emotions and purpose.

Have you ever fallen in love? Where you are so captivated by someone and want to spend all of your time with them? You may spend hours on end on the phone, or physically by their side. You want to know all their many layers. Not only do you want to know how their day was, but you also want to peel back the layers to know their dreams, their fears, their aspirations, the reason and purpose for their lives, as they seek to know the same about you. Those conversations where you exchange not only information, but also exchange deeper emotion. You have a child-like wonder to discover more. Those conversations that leave you feeling bonded at the heart, those are examples of transformational conversations.

Transformational conversations spark us to collaborate: they usually have a "share and discover"[53] dynamic, where family members are actively sharing information between one another and are working together toward discovery of new ideas to co-create solutions. People falling in love are similar. Not only do they actively share about their individual selves, they also have conversations exploring their future lives together, having joint dreams, visions, and plans. Just like lovers, family members need to be open and vulnerable to have transformational conversations, moving from "ask-tell" to "share and discover."

Transactional conversations are felt in the head, whereas transformational conversations are felt in the heart. Mastering the art of transformational conversation is necessary to building a connected family, as such conversations go beyond the intellectual to acknowledging the emotional. This requires two-way communication of emotions. Though it's a myth that 93% of human communication is non-verbal,[54] an extraordinary amount of emotions are communicated not only through words, but also through the face, eyes, and tone of voice. Therefore, deeper-level transformational conversations cannot really be had on the phone or virtually, they can only be had face to face.

The challenge is that it is increasingly difficult to have such conversations. Though we are in a fast-paced technological age, where our digital devices operate at lightning speed, our communications have seen an explosion in the volume of message exchange, at the expense of meaning exchange. Our fast-paced modern lives have given rise to time scarcity such that our interactions are more "efficient," with more tasks and decision-making being executed.

However, we are increasingly time-poor, with less time and space for emotions. This is worsened by the fact that our families are increasingly geographically dispersed, making face-to-face conversations a rarity. We may be better connected technologically, but we are less connected relationally.

Technology has enabled us to have more task-oriented conversations that are frequent in number. They have enabled a greater quantity of conversations, not necessarily greater-quality conversations. Arguably, technology has led to a decline in the quality of family conversations as family members are glued to their digital devices and struggle to unplug digitally to plug in relationally. Transformational conversations, unlike transactional conversations, require time. There needs to be an ease in the environment, to allow for family members to go deep, to have conversation on purpose, to acknowledge suppressed emotions, to share stories, and to ask questions. This cannot be done on the fly or under time pressure. While transformational conversations require an investment of time, they yield transformational impact: family members may find healing, new insights, and new awareness. Therefore, family members should invest time to exchange about the why, rather than just focusing on the what. To do so, they must make room for the head and the heart.

The Cadence of Transformational Conversations

Cadence means the "rhythm of sounds." Just as a marching band marches along to the rhythm set by the drummer, families also need to have transformational conversations in rhythm. Transformational conversations require intentionality. Just as a band will not be able to stay together without cadence, families will fail to stay connected without a plan. Thus, families need to intentionally plan out the frequency of their communications rather than be sporadic and unpredictable.

In addition to intentionally planning for the frequency of communications, families need to plan the flow. Certain environments are more conducive than others to allowing for transformational conversations. Transformational conversations happen best in an informal environment, outside of the boardroom. For example, they are more likely to happen at dinner tables or, even better, at remote locations on a retreat. In addition, not only do physical environments matter, the psychological environment is critical: transformational conversations only happen in an environment of safety.

Families that engage in transformational conversations are better connected. These conversations are like the life-blood of both connections up and connections across, keeping them vibrant. In addition, they enable synergies, such that families enjoy diversity of thought and co-creation of great ideas.

Enabling Transformational Conversations

Transformational conversations are not a given. They require the right conditions to yield: oneness of purpose, trust, transparency, openness, and vulnerability. These can be summed up as the 3Ps: purposefulness, psychological safety, and proximity. Thus, to create an enabling environment for transformational conversations, families need to focus on:

1) Being purposeful, to understand our common purpose
2) Nurturing psychological safety to foster trust, transparency, and vulnerability
3) Having emotional proximity, to develop understanding of one another.

In the next three chapters I will unpack each of the 3Ps.

CHAPTER 19

Purpose

The first time I heard Simon Sinek speak on a TED Talk, How Great Leaders Inspire Action, I was simply blown away. Sinek observed that all great leaders had a lot in common: they think, act, and communicate in a way that is the opposite of other leaders. He explained his "Golden Circle" model: three concentric circles with WHY in the inside, followed by HOW in the middle and WHAT on the outside.

Sinek found that great leaders have clarity of why—their purpose, their cause, their belief, the reason for the existence of their organizations, and why others should care. They think, act, and communicate from the inside out of the Golden Circle. Other leaders focus on the WHAT, i.e. the things they need to do, and the HOW, i.e. how they need to do it, but often lack clarity of the WHY. Consequently, most leaders tend to think, act, and communicate from the outside in.

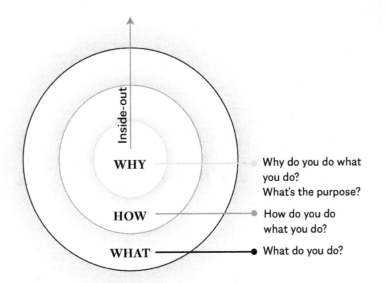

Simon's clarion call is for leaders and their organizations to start with WHY: he argues that exceptional companies such as Apple and Walmart have a cutting edge because they start with the WHY. Simon explains that this is hardwired in our human biology: the Golden Circle matches the way our brains work.

The neocortex is the part of the brain responsible for rational and analytical thought. It enables us to synthesize large numbers of facts and figures, but it is not responsible for behavior. The limbic brain, on the other hand, is responsible for emotions like trust and loyalty, and this part of the brain is responsible for all behavior and decision-making. Our neocortex corresponds with the WHAT, whereas our limbic corresponds with the WHY and HOW.

The implication is that when companies start with WHY, they are able to tap into the innate human drive to want to belong and to be loyal to the company. Customers then see the

WHAT as an extension of their values and beliefs. People do not buy what companies do or how they do it, they buy WHY they do it. Starting with WHY is scientific.

The implication of Sinek's finding is also significant for you as a family enterprise owner. Family members are not compelled by what the enterprise does or how it does it, they are compelled by WHY it does it. Having an understanding of a deeper purpose of the family enterprise gives family members a compelling cause to rally around. You need to start with WHY.

Applying the Golden Circle

Applying the Golden Circle to a family business context means that as an owner, you need to understand firstly WHY you own what you own, then HOW to own what you own, and lastly WHAT precisely you own. The WHY speaks to an exploration of identity whereas the HOW and WHAT speak to exploration of technicality. The identity is more important than the technicality.

The challenge is that, historically, little thought may have gone into the WHY. Instead, your business may have been created to put food on the table to provide for family members. Over the years it may have evolved, becoming larger than life, generating wealth for many beneficiaries. A lot of focus may have been on the WHAT, e.g. driving revenue, growing profits, and diversifying wealth; and on the HOW, e.g. attracting and retaining talent, strategic initiatives, and raising capital.

In addition, your enterprise may have evolved in scope, from having just one operating business to having several businesses as well as other investment assets. Your focus, however, may have been on WHAT you own in the enterprise and HOW to own it, as opposed to WHY you own it. For instance, there may have been focus on legal structuring, estate planning, and investment management, as opposed to stepping back to understand why you collectively own these assets. As Sinek identified, thinking from the outside in will not create an exceptional family enterprise. Instead, you need to think from the inside out, starting with purpose.

As Napoleon Hill said, "There is one quality that one must possess to win, and that is definiteness of purpose, the knowledge of what one wants, and a burning desire to possess it."

Definiteness of Purpose

To win as a family business owner, you need to have definiteness of purpose. It is that definiteness of purpose that serves as a fuel to chase after the WHAT. So, what is purpose? It is "the reason for which something is created or which something exists." You get clear on the purpose of the family enterprise by understanding its cause, what the family believes in, and what your raison d'être is. Purpose acts like a glue, creating cohesion within the family and the enterprise. It is this deeper purpose that the family vision, mission, and values hinge upon.

As we navigate generational transitions, the importance of definiteness of shared purpose is critical. Our families' mindsets need to shift from "me" (founder-driven) to "we" (family-driven), as it transitions into a sibling partnership. In absence of this shift, family members may venture in different directions and not be on the same page. Individuals can opt to pursue independent enterprise, as opposed to an interdependent family enterprise.

Therefore, it is important that the definiteness of purpose is a collective one, where your entire family collectively defines it, gaining clarity on the answers to the questions "WHY do we own what we own TOGETHER?", "What's the compelling reason for us to stay as owners TOGETHER?", and "HOW do we stay as owners TOGETHER?"

Shared purpose goes beyond just the operating business, it also incorporates the family office or family foundation. For business families, financial considerations are typically important, but non-financial considerations are equally important. For example, while families may seek to provide financial security for the family, they also typically seek to uphold a good reputation, to give back to the local community, to nurture stakeholder relationships, to have family harmony, and to leave a lasting legacy. Thus, the shared purposes in family enterprises are rarely purely financial or purely emotional. They are usually a combination of the two.

The late Myles Munroe said, "Where purpose is not known, abuse is inevitable." Lacking clarity of purpose leads to abuse, particularly as we make generational transitions. The founder may intuitively know the purpose of the enterprise, but as we have more family members becoming actively engaged, it is critical to actively define and agree on this purpose. The danger of not doing so is that family members become entitled—they demand benefits that are not proportionate to their contributions, and may lack respect for all that it took to build the enterprise to its level of success. Their mentality toward the family wealth may be "let's blow it" or "let's show it," as opposed to "let's steward it" or "let's multiply it." To circumvent such abuse, it is critical that we get clear on the reason for the existence of the enterprise, defining its purpose.

The Third Eye

In Sanskrit, chakra is known as the "seat of intuition," also known as the "third eye." The idea is that the third eye allows for clear thought, contemplation, and self-reflection. It helps one to determine one's reality and beliefs based on one's choices. It governs self-awareness, wisdom, visualization, and creative dreaming. As a family business owner, it's important to open your third eye, to be more conscious so that you can create the future that you want to see for yourself and for your family. To do so, you have to become more conscious of the nuances of your family, and be conscious of what family means in your household.

It's important to know who is defined as a family member for the purpose of the family enterprise. Who will you be considering as beneficial owners and/or decision-makers? Defining family as an African can be philosophical, as often our concept of family is fluid and non-scientific.

Many of us have sisters, brothers, aunties, uncles, and grandparents who are not related to us by blood or marriage. These are non-family family. Similarly, in some polygamous homes, "family" refers to Dad, Mom and Dad and Mom's joint children, whereas in others, it refers to the wider unit including all the wives and their respective children. Then there's the subject of in-laws: some families consider them as immediate family whereas others do not.

In addition to the complexity of the family unit, our families are often influenced by multiple cultures, as we may have inter-ethnic homes. With over 3,000 tribes on the continent, the diversity of culture can bring about diversity in the modus operandi of our individual families. Some of our nuclear households are strongly delineated from the extended family as typically observed in individualist cultures, whereas others are more fluid and dependent on extended family members as in collectivist cultures. In such families, uncles, aunts, cousins, and grandparents may be considered as immediate stakeholders and decision-makers.

It's important to be conscious of the dynamics in your family and have clarity.

Why This, Why Us, Why Now?

Beverly Knight was one of my favorite soul singers as a teenager. I would listen to her album on my mini-disc player on the way to school and back. One track in particular stood out, titled "Why me, why you, why now?" In the song, Beverly is reminiscing on a failed relationship, asking these three powerful questions: Why me? Why you? Why now? These powerful questions can be applied to those on a journey to discover purpose.

After getting clear on who is considered family for the purpose of the family enterprise, it is important to then get clear on the enterprise's big WHY, by answering the three categories of questions:

- Why this (enterprise)?
- Why us (as an owning family)?
- Why now (what purpose are we fulfilling at this point in time)?

This involves reflecting on the following questions:

Enterprise:
- What is our purpose as an enterprising family?
- What is the purpose of this enterprise for the family?

Family:
- What is our purpose as a family?
- What does it mean to be a family in business?
- What does it mean to be an investing family?
- What is the purpose of the family for the enterprise?

Now:
- Has our purpose changed over time? Does it need to change?

The family purpose can be considered as a snapshot in time, i.e. it reflects the purpose of the family at a given point in time. It is not meant to be static; rather, it is to be dynamic, evolving as the family, industry, family capital, and the world evolves. This dynamism is important to be able to engage the rising generation, so that they are energized and enthused by it. In addition, it is important to be relevant.

Therefore, it is important to periodically revisit the shared purpose and consider whether it needs to be amended by expansion, deletion, or change in scope. Family members need to have a dynamic mindset, being adjustable, adaptable, and agile as they jointly craft the shared purpose. In doing so, they craft an enterprise that embraces change—an enterprise that is future-focused and not past-focused.

French writer Antoine de Saint-Exupery said, "If you want to build a ship, don't herd people together to collect wood and don't assign them tasks and work, but rather teach them to long for the endless immensity of the sea."

By teaching your family members to embrace a dynamic mindset, you are encouraging them to long for the endless immensity of the sea as opposed to being focused on tasks.

From We to Me

Once you have clarity of a shared purpose, it is key to not only announce the purpose, but to also create opportunities for family members to connect with it and experience it. This enables you to see how connected they individually are with the purpose, and also how interconnected they are with one another in serving the wider purpose, going from we to me.

I remember as a child in primary school reciting the national pledge every day in assembly after singing the national anthem. These were words I had crammed and could rote off by heart, but could not explain what they meant or the relevance they had in my life! We would say:

I pledge to Nigeria my country,
To be faithful, loyal and honest,
To serve Nigeria with all my strength,
To defend her unity, and uphold her honor and glory,
So help me God.

I couldn't tell you what it meant to be faithful, loyal, and serve Nigeria nor could I tell you how I personally would demonstrate faithfulness, loyalty, and servitude to Nigeria as a six-year-old. No one had ever explained that to me, or modeled out this pledge in action, and so honestly I never truly cared! Instead, my focus was on making sure I remembered the pledge so that I would not be punished by my teacher for reciting it incorrectly.

Often, citizens are like me; they recite national pledges as rituals, but they do not truly feel a sense of patriotism or loyalty to their nations. This is because, like me, they may not have stopped to reflect on the deeper meaning and significance of the pledge and how it applies to them as individuals. A similar phenomenon may prevail in business families, whereby individuals feel no sense of connection to the overall shared purpose.

To avoid purpose becoming hollow and without meaning, it is important that we give individuals sufficient time to reflect on the relevance and application to themselves. This is so that they are able to connect the dots from we to me. Defining a compelling collective purpose is insufficient; it must connect to each individual, looking at each individual's strengths, passions, motivators, and areas of interest, and seeing how it attaches to the collective purpose.

This connecting of the dots from "we to me" takes the concept of the family purpose from abstract to practical, as each individual evaluates how they can contribute to the collective purpose, answering "What are our individual purposes and how do they fit into the wider collective purpose?" This enables members to not only have legal citizenry but also emotional citizenry. This allows for family members to feel connected, understanding how they contribute to the larger purpose, regardless of how large or small their role is.

Engaging family members requires an understanding of where they thrive and what drives them. In other words, what are their strengths and their motivators? A great tool to use is Clifton Strengths Assessment by Gallup. It is a personality test that uncovers each family member's strengths and motivations as well as the family's collective strengths and motivations. This enables you to jointly determine which roles and responsibilities would be optimal for each family member. In addition, the tool unveils areas for development for both individuals and the collective team, enabling you to prepare customized development plans for each family member. It's powerful, allowing for greater self-awareness and team awareness.

Definiteness of shared purpose is critical for business families that seek to cross the generational bridge. It allows for the development of intrinsic motivation, where family members are driven internally to care about the family enterprise. This leads to the development of emotional ownership, and not just legal ownership of the enterprise, such that all family members are actively engaged in the family enterprise.

CHAPTER 20

Creating Psychological Safety

I Belong Here

When I first started my speaking career, I suffered from big-time imposter syndrome. While on stage, I would be confronted by all sorts of self-sabotaging thoughts, saying "You can't do this," "Why are you qualified for this," "They'll soon find out you're a fraud," and the worst of all, "There's no room for YOU here." I focused on what I believed were my disqualifiers—my age, my race, and my gender, as unfortunately there were very few people that looked like me in my industry. I was afraid that I would not be well received. I was scared that I would be ridiculed.

I lacked safety. Stepping out on stage made me feel very vulnerable. What I desired was the assurance that I would not be ridiculed. It took me some time to recognize that I had to provide that safety for myself by affirming myself. Instead of focusing on my disqualifiers, I had to remind myself that I was qualified. Thereafter, I would give myself a pep talk before getting on stage, repeating "I belong here." As a result, I felt confident enough to embrace the stage and share my message.

We all hate feeling othered, where we do not fit in within the norms of a given social group. This may be because of our age, gender, race, political affiliations, or religion. This feeling emanates where safety is lacking. In my case, I lacked safety within. In some cases, others lack safety without, i.e. safety not provided by external parties. Where there is safety (within or without), we begin to feel a sense of belonging and then feel comfortable sharing our messages—our ideas, questions, perspectives, mistakes, and emotions. Where there is safety, we are assured that as we share our messages, we will not be booed off the stage, but rather will be cheered by the audience.

Similarly, where there is psychological safety, people feel comfortable sharing their ideas. Not only do they feel comfortable sharing, but they also are enabled to take risks, to challenge the status quo, and to fail. They are permitted to "Voice half-finished thoughts, ask questions out of left field, and brainstorm out loud in order to create a culture that truly innovates."[55]

So, What Is Psychological Safety?

Psychological safety is a term coined by Dr. Amy Edmonson of Harvard University. In her study, Dr. Edmonson discovered that a team's performance is dependent on its members' beliefs about personal interaction and whether they have "A shared belief held by members of a team that the team is safe for interpersonal risk taking".[56] She defines it as "A belief that one will not be punished or humiliated for speaking up with ideas, questions, concerns or mistakes."

Psychological safety enables groups to generate collaborative intelligence. There is overwhelming evidence pointing to the fact that groups with diverse teams benefit from diversity of thought. Groups that consist of people with different experiences bring different perspectives and are able to not only identify problems but also co-create better solutions than non-diverse groups. This is due to cognitive diversity.

Cognitive diversity is diversity of thought, values, and personalities, and it has been found to increase team innovation by up to 20%.[57] This is because diversity usually leads to better decision-making and adaptability. These gains from diversity are not automatic though. There must be psychological safety to shift the power dynamics of the team, so that all team members feel comfortable to move from being observers to being contributors. They must move from seeing themselves as an other, to being part of the fold. They must move from co-existing to co-creating.

The resulting impact of connected teams is phenomenal. Teams that are not only diverse but also inclusive are able to have transformational impact. They are able to adapt, they are able to attract and retain talent, and they are able to deliver stronger financial performance. A Deloitte study on diversity and inclusion found that an increase in individuals' feelings of inclusion leads to an increase of 17% in team performance, 20% in decision-making quality, and 29% in collaboration.[58]

A case in point is Qantas, an Australian airline that in 2013 was posting record losses of $2.8 billion. By 2017, the business had turned around to deliver record profits of $850 million. The business was in the top quartile of its global industry and was ranked as Australia's most attractive employer! The CEO attributed this transformation to diversity and inclusion.

This equally applies in family enterprises. Often, families are divided along the lines of age, gender, and family tribe, limiting connection. The irony is that, unlike businesses, families are naturally endowed with diversity (age and gender) and so have the greatest potential for transformation. Unfortunately, families are not necessarily inclusive. To maximize the gains from diversity, family members need to move from co-existing to connecting: those who see themselves as an other must reorient to seeing themselves as part of the fold. There must be safety within and without to share their messages.

A consequence of these better connections is a greater ability of the family enterprise to transform: like Qantas, families become more adaptable, agile, and able to withstand internal or external disruptions, delivering stronger financial performance. Not only are they able to transform, but they are also able to be transformational. They are able to cultivate business models and ideas that generate lasting value to their customers, they are more effective at deploying family capital to generate social returns, and they are able to have greater impact in their communities. In short, they are able to leave lasting legacies.

To realize this immense potential, there must be a conducive environment that allows for contribution from all family members. The challenge is, despite this natural advantage that families have, they often have established patterns that implicitly determine power dynamics, and these dynamics do not provide a level playing field for all members to actively contribute. These patterns are strongly influenced by culture, society, and religion.

For example, many African cultures are elder-dominant, where elders are not to be questioned and are to make all decisions. In addition, many cultures are patriarchal. The implication of this is that young family members and female family members may feel that they are not licensed to have a voice and/or that they are not permitted to have a voice. The consequence of this is that the founder may continue dominating in providing solutions.

This comes at a huge disadvantage to the family enterprise as "Innovation is almost always a collaborative process and almost never a lightbulb moment of lone genius."[59] The family misses out on a collaborative process where ideas are shared and discovered, rather than relying on the lone genius of the founder. The gains from the diversity of the family unit are therefore not automatic. To maximize the gains of diversity in the family, we must build psychological safety.

The Stages of Psychological Safety

Dr. Timothy Clark, author of The 4 Stages of Psychological Safety: Defining the Path to Inclusion and Innovation, has identified four key stages of psychological safety. In his model, he explains that it is only until members of a team progress through all stages that they feel "safe" to contribute and challenge the status quo. When they have progressed through all four stages, we see the full benefits of diversity.

Stage 1: Inclusion Safety
This refers to the need to belong. Liz Follien said, "Diversity

is having a seat at the table, inclusion is having a voice, and belonging is having that voice be heard."

Where there is inclusion safety, team members are included such that they feel the courage to stand alone like leopards, as opposed to wanting to camouflage like chameleons. They have the courage to stand alone, to feel safe being themselves, and to showcase their unique attributes and characteristics.

Stage 2: Learner Safety

This refers to the need to learn and develop. With inclusion safety, team members may proudly stand alone but may be stagnant in their personal growth.

In contrast, where there is learner safety, members ask questions, give and receive feedback, take risks, and "fail." In addition, they have the humility to learn from others.

Stage 3: Contributor Safety

Contributor safety satisfies the need to make a difference. Whereas learning is uni-directional (i.e. members are receiving insights, perspectives, and knowledge), contribution is bi-directional, where members are also contributing their insights, perspectives and knowledge.

Where there is contributor safety, members enjoy autonomy, independence, confidence, and fulfillment.

Stage 4: Challenger Safety

Challenger safety satisfies the need to make things better. Under contributor safety, members may contribute their ideas but not necessarily challenge the status quo.

Where there is challenger safety, members feel safe to speak up and challenge without fear of punishment, ostracism, or reputation damage. Challenger safety allows for disagreement and debate.

Families that desire the greatest diversity of thought need to foster all four tenets of psychological safety to accelerate learning, increase contribution and performance, and stimulate innovation.

This all sounds great in theory but often can be uncomfortable as it requires you to confront your deeply held beliefs and values: in the words of Dr. Clark, it requires you to "crack yourself open" and ask yourself some difficult questions. It's important to note that the nurturing of psychological safety is not the nurturing of psychological comfort, as often you will get deeply uncomfortable!

You need to ask yourself whether you truly believe that:

- All family members are equal regardless of their age, race, gender, tribe, etc.
- All family members are to learn and grow and should be supported in this journey, even as they make mistakes or lack confidence
- All family members are to be granted autonomy to contribute in their own way
- All family members have the license to challenge the status quo to make things better

If you do, you can foster these four tenets of safety by engaging in the following activities.

Reflecting and addressing

There are often biases in families that hinder inclusivity. For example, a family may have developed a bias against including women in enterprise matters or to default to the eldest son as the successor. These biases may become deeply embedded in the family culture.

Sometimes, these biases are by design and reflect the values of the family; however, other times these biases are by default "inherited" and passed from generation to generation. The collective bias is also a function of individual family members' biases.

Thus, it is critical that you take time to reflect, to identify any unconscious and conscious biases you may hold, and then you can address them. Addressing these biases involves including all members in decision-making and asking for their input, thoughts, and feedback. It involves accepting "outsiders" into the fold. This requires you to develop a learner's mindset to be open to new perspectives and ideas.

Learner's mindset

Key to developing psychological safety is curiosity. Curiosity is an openness to what is new, and a readiness for exploration and innovation. It involves a childlike quality of wonder, openness, and playfulness. It means being able to suspend or place to one side your fixed notions and see the world in new ways and from other perspectives. It helps you understand other people and different perceptions, and thus to effect change.

It helps you to consider alternatives, internally questioning your own fixed mindsets and habits. Instead of fixed mindsets, curious people have learners' mindsets. This is where they seek to be perpetual students and not teachers. It is this curiosity that keeps family members open-minded, humble, and teachable.

As Alvin Toffler said, "The illiterate of the 21st century will not be those who cannot read or write, but those who cannot learn, unlearn and relearn."

Family members are students who have the ability to not only learn new ideas, perspectives, and insights but also unlearn unhelpful ones and relearn useful ones. As learners, members are able to shed biases that hinder inclusivity.

Key to developing curiosity is learning the skill of asking questions. Family members should seek to be like journalists, who ask questions without judgment or presuppositions about the right answers, and not be like teachers who ask students questions with answers in mind that they judge while marking the scripts.

In asking without judgment or presupposition, they cultivate an environment where there is learner safety, such that all family members are empowered to learn.

Active listening

Communication involves not just delivery of messages but also receipt of messages. However, emphasis is often placed on ensuring that the sender projects a clear message, rather than on the receiver being patient enough to decode the message. When messages are not decoded, the receiver lacks understanding; they may have heard the message but have not listened. With active listening comes understanding.

Communication is a two-way street, with equal responsibility on both the sender and listener to ensure that messages are clearly delivered. To effectively understand messages, active deep listening must be practiced by receivers, so that they not only hear messages but also listen to them. Families need to be attentive while their loved ones speak, and listen without judgment.

Listening to understand (rather than to respond) is key. This is particularly critical where there is a power imbalance between the receiver and the sender. For instance, consider a young female family member communicating an emotive matter to her older father in a household that is highly elder-dominant and patriarchal. The daughter may be intimidated by the position of her father as she seeks to get vulnerable on matters of her heart. It is critical that her father actively listens so that she feels safe.

Ways one can practice active deep listening:

- Not being distracted: making eye contact as the speaker speaks and not using devices
- Actively engaging: displaying feedback that one is listening through verbal and non-verbal communication, asking follow-up questions and asking for clarification where necessary
- Being patient and not interrupting.

As a result of active listening, trust develops between the listener and the speaker, and the sender is validated. This validation enables the speaker to contribute their insights, perspectives, and knowledge.

Creating a Culture of Challenging

In order to cultivate challenger safety, we must develop a culture of challenging. This can be done by embracing vulnerability as a skill. Vulnerability is uncomfortable and requires exposing oneself to the possibility of harm, loss, or rejection. This can be embraced by modeling it to other family business owners through the sharing of failures. Allow family members to use these failures as a case study, to understand the decisions you made that led to said failures, so that they can challenge them and learn from them.

This normalizes uncertainty and opens up their mindsets toward being vulnerable. In addition, it normalizes challenging decision-making. Not only will they challenge historic decisions, but they also develop the skill to challenge current and future decisions in the family enterprise.

This can be reinforced by systemizing challenger questions in family meetings. Questions can be asked that challenge the status quo, the aim of which is to provoke discussion among the family. This creates a culture of challenging the status quo and allows members to envision new possibilities and form new hypotheses as they think outside the box. You may choose to assign a dedicated "challenger" per family meeting, who will ask a challenger question. The challenger can rotate among family members, to benefit from cognitive diversity.

Lastly, a culture of challenging can be developed by creating a culture of healthy debate. This normalizes diverse views, allowing for family members to debate issues based on their pros and cons.

As a result of nurturing psychological safety, your family

allows for greater understanding of each other on a cognitive level; you are able to observe how you each interpret, perceive, and evaluate knowledge. In doing so, you build the cognitive intelligence of the collective unit.

The Safety to Heal

Not only does psychological safety allow for exploration of the intellectual, it also allows for exploration of the emotional. When a family creates a culture of psychological safety, not only do they benefit from diversity of thought, they also benefit from acknowledgement and potential healing from suppressed emotions.

The term "holding space" is commonly used by therapists. It essentially means psychological safety, applied to a context of emotions. In the words of Heather Plett, it means:

> *We are willing to walk alongside another person in whatever journey they're on without judging them, making them feel inadequate, trying to fix them, or trying to impact the outcome. When we hold space for other people, we open our hearts, offer unconditional support, and let go of judgement and control."*

When space is held effectively, not only do family members feel that their persons belong, they also feel that their emotions belong, whether positive or negative. There is no judgment whatsoever. They feel that they are in the company of a trusted friend, with whom they can share their "secrets." They are then able to open up and confide, expressing emotions such as anxiety, fear, and shame. They are able to have difficult conversations about death, money, and wealth.

The family moves from being an avenue through which they can express their highest intellectual selves, to an avenue where they can unveil their fullest emotional selves. It becomes a safe space to have conversations on pain, regret, fear, and shame and thus acknowledge and address trauma. It becomes an avenue for deep conversation, authenticity, and vulnerability. This empowers connection with one another, heightened awareness, inner transformation, and healing.

As Maryam Hasnaa said:

> A healer does not heal you. A healer is someone who holds space for you while you awaken your inner healer, so that you may heal yourself."

CHAPTER 21

The Importance of Emotional Proximity

A couple of years ago, I received an inquiry from Kafiyat, a family business owner who had been working alongside her mother for two years. Her mother, Bimbo, was the founder of a furniture manufacturing company that had been established 20 years prior. After graduating from University, Kafiyat worked in a consulting firm for two years. She then decided to join the family business, and worked as the human resources manager for five years. However, when Kafiyat called me, she was at the end of her tether and had sent her mom a resignation letter.

The mother-daughter duo kept arguing over the direction of the business and the culture, so much so that they would have screaming matches in the office. Kafiyat felt that her mom was too controlling. Everything started and ended with her. She said that she was also sentimental and informal with the staff: many of them lacked formal titles and job descriptions. In addition, they were not rewarded based on their productivity. On the other hand, Bimbo felt Kafiyat lacked understanding of what it took to build the business over the years. Many of these staff whom Kafiyat snubbed were laboring there from the beginning, contributing to its current success.

Kafiyat called me, really upset. She was adamant that she would not be returning to the business. However, she was worried about how the severance of her employment would affect her personal relationship with her mom. She noted that she and her mom were no longer close; their interactions would usually end in verbal fights. These fights followed them home, where her father, siblings, and extended family would try to intervene, albeit unsuccessfully. She did not know what to do to move forward.

I explained to Kafiyat that she and her mother had different perspectives, priorities, and preferences, and in order to move forward she would have to move closer in heart to her mom and see things the way she did. Bimbo was not university educated; she began trading fabrics in her mid-20s with financial support from her father at first. Kafiyat, on the other hand, went to university in Cardiff where she studied psychology, and she had worked in a corporation. Their understanding of business was completely different.

Kafiyat explained that her mom incessantly complained that she was not appreciative of her. I explained that Mom desired affirmation from her only girl. She wanted Kafiyat to be proud of all that she had accomplished, especially as a female entrepreneur who flourished against the odds. The business had evolved from its humble beginnings in just textile trading, to having two additional business lines including manufacturing and real estate. Kafiyat, in her zeal to make a positive change by professionalizing, came across as a foe and not a friend. Thus, Mom and Daughter were unable to see eye to eye and there was a complete breakdown in their working relationship.

"Ahhhhhh, I wish I had known this all this time!" Kafiyat said, "I now understand the way she sees things and why we were not on the same page." Kafiyat had been unaware of her mom's perspective and her mom was equally unaware of hers. The conflicts all arose because both Mom and Daughter lacked emotional connectedness, and thus lacked the ability to understand the feelings of one another. They lacked empathy.

What Is Empathy?

Empathy is the ability to step into the shoes of another person and feel their emotions. It is the ability to understand and share the feelings of others. When one is empathetic, one is able to imagine what the next person might be feeling or thinking.

In the blog post "Empathy: Not Such a Soft Skill," in Harvard Business Review, editor Katherine Bell writes:

> It's an act of imagination in which you try to look at the world from the perspective of another person, a human being whose history and point of view are as complex as your own. At all levels of management, empathy is a critical skill. If you can imagine a person's point of view—no matter what you think of it—you can more effectively influence him."

Thus, leaders who are able to demonstrate empathy can influence more effectively. In addition to influence, another consequence of empathy is "emotional proximity",[60] which is a greater level of emotional connectedness. Families like Kafiyat's can gain a greater understanding of each other on an emotional level by developing empathy. They can seek to draw close to one another not only in body, but also in mind.

There are three different types of empathy: affective, somatic, and cognitive. Affective is the ability to understand another person's emotions. Somatic is having a physical reaction in response to what someone else is experiencing. Cognitive empathy is the ability to understand another person's mental state and thoughts in a given situation. In a family enterprise, the key empathies to develop are affective and cognitive empathy, so that members can "get" each other on both an intellectual and an emotional level.

One of my absolute favorite quotes is by Stephen Covey: "Seek first to understand and then to be understood" from his book *The 7 Habits of Highly Effective People*. Covey explains that empathy is key to building relationships. When others feel understood by you, they are more likely to be receptive to your ideas. We must demonstrate an understanding of their situation, their pains and gains, before we can start to provide solutions. We can seek to understand by observing them. We are seeking to understand not just their minds, but also their hearts. We are seeking to build both affective and cognitive empathy.

Empathy Mapping

Empathy mapping is a useful tool for gaining deeper insight into one another. While it is commonly used by businesses to gain a deeper understanding of potential consumers, its application is also relevant in the context of families. It was first developed by Dave Gray and it is widely used in agile and design communities.

The use of empathy mapping can bring about greater emotional proximity in families, as there are often distances across generations, genders, and family tribes, and focusing too much on these differences can hinder collaboration. Empathy maps can act as bridge builders; they enable family members to gain a deeper understanding of each other, across generations and within generations.

I was listening to a podcast by Jay Shetty recently, and Will Smith was the guest. Will explained that his experience as an actor has been invaluable, as it taught him how to develop a deep understanding of other people's perspectives. If he has to play a character who believes something that he personally doesn't believe in, he has to uproot all his personal beliefs and implant new ideas to be able to bring the character to life.

Often in families we don't always share the same beliefs as our loved ones: Kafiyat and Bimbo for example had divergent views on how to manage the business. In order to develop empathy for one another, we should learn to be like actors. Like Will Smith, we should also develop the skill of uprooting our beliefs and implanting the new ideas and perspectives of our family members. We should learn to not be so grounded in our individual beliefs that we are unable to embrace another person's character, and instead see life through the same lens through which they see. It is when we are able to perfect this that we are able to bring their character to life and prepare an accurate empathy map.

This requires us to observe and not judge our family

members. It requires us to be neutral, and receptive to cues. It requires us to be unbiased, not influenced by previous information, emotion, and attitudes we may have toward a given family member. It requires suspending all judgment and exploring one's mind. It requires us to listen and not just hear, listening with our ears and with our hearts.

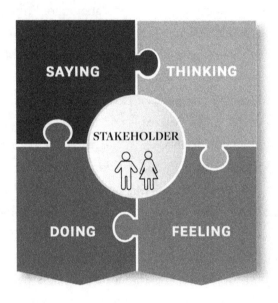

Developing the Empathy Map

The goal of the empathy map is to gain a deep understanding of your family member across the four quadrants: thinking, feeling, doing, and saying.

Thinking

The thinking quadrant captures what the family member is thinking with respect to the family enterprise. Here, you are trying to gauge what occupies their thoughts, and what matters to them. Sometimes this is not easily observable and is not vocalized by the family member; it could be deeply emotive and they may not be ready to share. For example, Bimbo may have been dealing with shame. Equally, Kafiyat may have been dealing with fear of the future and/or stewardship anxiety. Both family members may have been self-conscious and afraid to share all their thoughts.

Feeling

The feeling quadrant captures what the family member's emotional state is. Here, you are trying to understand what worries them, what excites them, and what they feel about the family enterprise.

Doing

The doing quadrant captures what the family member is inclined to do with respect to the family enterprise. This captures both their formal role (e.g. chair of the family business) and their informal role. An in-law may not have a formal role in the family enterprise but may have significant influence over their spouse. It's important to have a deep understanding of both the tasks that family members carry out, and the influence that they have over others.

Saying

The saying quadrant contains what the family member verbally expresses about the family enterprise, their desire or fear about it, for instance.

Human beings are complex, and often there may be supposed inconsistencies across the quadrants; family members may express both positive and negative emotions about the enterprise. Your role is to use these as cues to uncover deeper insights about your loved ones. It is your role to investigate the cause of the inconsistency and seek to resolve it.

In addition, there are often many overlaps between the quadrants. If you have any quadrants with no information, that's a sign that you need to spend more time observing and perhaps asking questions.

Such questions may include:

- What do they see in their immediate environment? What do they see others saying and doing? What are they watching and reading?
- What decisions do they need to make? What will trigger them to be successful, and how can we find out if they've succeeded?
- What do their family, friends, colleagues, and other stakeholders say about the family enterprise?
- What do they fear? Are they frustrated, anxious, or worried about their present situation? Identify their pain points. Then, identify their gains, their dreams, and hopes. What do they want? What are their pains and gains?

The mapping exercise enables you to build empathy with your family members.

Speaking in a Language that Is Native

In "The 5 Love Languages," Gary Chapman hypothesizes that we each have a "native" love language that is our preference to receive as well as express love in. He further explains that what tends to happen in relationships is that each partner typically expresses love in their own native language, but this language may be foreign to the other partner. As a result, they fail to understand one another, and this communication clash can create conflict, eroding the quality of the relationship.

Similarly in families, each family member has different priorities, perspectives, and preferences, which influence the way they think, feel, see, speak, hear, and fear. They are likened to speaking unique languages. For example, Bimbo had a desire to keep the business informal, with staff being treated like family, whereas Kafiyat had a desire to professionalize. If we fail to understand each other's languages, we are unable to communicate in our family member's native language. This leads to a lack of understanding of one another, and tension.

It is important to speak to your family members in the language that they understand. The information uncovered in the empathy map is invaluable, as you can use it appropriately. For instance, Kafiyat may have uncovered that Bimbo's aspiration is to grow profits of the enterprise over the medium run. She may also have uncovered that she is dealing with anticipatory grief with respect to letting go of the enterprise.

Now armed with this information, she can use it to enable her to speak to her mom in a language that she will understand. The language Bimbo understands is increasing profits; anything outside of that is incomprehensible. Kafiyat, on the other hand, may have a desire to introduce a technology software across the family operating business. In communicating to her mom, it is important to focus on relevancy not technicality. Relevancy speaks to how the introduction of the software would achieve her mom's primary objectives, whereas technicality speaks to details on the functionality of the software. By focusing on relevancy, she is able to connect the dots from her idea to her mom's goals, perhaps by focusing on how the technology would yield improved productivity and thus an increase in profit.

Being a Teacher, Not a Preacher

Another way of saying this is to be a teacher, not a preacher. Preachers often focus on a message of salvation as the only way to heaven, but in doing so they can be moralizing. They may display expert knowledge of religious text, which can be not only intimidating but also unrelatable. Consequently, the congregation perceives a gap in "spiritual maturity" and is not inspired to take action. Instead of preaching, teach. Like preachers, teachers are experts, but they are able to provide age-appropriate learning. They recognize that in order for education to be effective, it must match the maturity of the student. As a result, they are adaptable in their delivery of lessons, and their students are better able to learn.

Often, as custodians of ideas, we are likened to experts, as we have spent so long stewing in our ideas and thoughts, whereas our other family members are like newbies. It's important that we are able to communicate ideas to them, rather than at them, inspiring insight, knowledge, understanding, action, and ownership. It is important to meet them where they are and adapt the delivery of the lessons so that they are appropriate. In absence of doing so, the knowledge and information remains useless, going over their heads. Sometimes, the knowledge and information irritates them, as they feel misunderstood.

In addition to what is being said, care has to be taken as to how it is being said. Having identified that Bimbo is dealing with shame, it's important that Kafiyat is not tone-deaf, but shows sensitivity. Using positive communication in addition to negative communication is helpful, reinforcing and praising positive actions or outcomes, rather than highlighting and emphasizing negative actions or outcomes.

Further, mirroring is useful in demonstrating empathy. For example, Kafiyat may say, "I can understand that you feel XYZ," or "I understand that you are concerned about ABC." This helps them to feel seen and heard and to reduce defensiveness. It is only when people feel seen and heard that they then see and hear. Speak sensitively, choosing your words carefully, speaking with grace.

Sharing Stories

Another valuable tool to use in developing empathy is storytelling. Often in families, members lack understanding of each other's stories. They may know the chronological observable history of their family members, but lack understanding of significant events that shaped them emotionally. Storytelling can help family members to get to know each other more emotionally and understand each other's values, visions and motivations.

To gain insight into each other's stories, each family member can engage in a timeline exercise, where they share with their family members significant events in their lives that have influenced them. The exercise provides the individual doing the exercise as well as the other family members with a bird eye's view of their lives, facilitating better understanding of both themselves and one another.

Using our earlier example, Kafiyat may be unaware that her mother encountered financial difficulties along her entrepreneurship journey. She had taken a loan from a bank to finance expansion at inception of the manufacturing business, and the business had not grown as quickly as she'd anticipated, leading to defaults on the loan. As a result, the business went bankrupt, and Bimbo had to start from scratch. Knowledge of this significant event would aid Kafiyat in knowing her mother better. It may provide clues as to why she is struggling to let go.

The timeline exercise enables both the individual and other family members to understand:

- Consistent themes that cut across different events of their lives
- Growth opportunities, lessons learned, and wisdom gleaned
- The thread between their present, past, and future
- How life experiences prepared them for future challenges
- How events have shaped their characters
- The interconnectivity between one another

The exercise allows for heightened consciousness, and deeper awareness of self and your family members. It not only allows insight into your personal development but also insight into the evolution of the family enterprise. It allows for cumulative wisdom gained by your family unit—through the triumphs and trials of both individuals and the enterprise itself—to be consciously identified, defined, and transmitted from your generation to the next generation. This wisdom is invaluable and can become the platform on which the next generation soars.

Creating a Lifeline

Here's how to create a lifeline, step by step.

1) Think of all the significant events that have shaped your entire life.
2) Note three of the most significant positive events and three of the most negative events.
3) Reflect on them.
4) Are there any consistent patterns emerging?
5) What did those events teach you?
6) How did the individual events influence future character or events you went through?

CHAPTER 22

Taking the First Step

I f you have not yet taken steps to build a connected family, you haven't missed your opportunity. The truth is: the sooner you take action, the sooner you'll see results. An African proverb says, "If you want to know the end, look at the beginning." This means that you have to be intentional and plan today so that you can reach your desired future destination.

The thought of taking the step can seem overwhelming. Having conversations on topics that you may have never had as a family may make you uncomfortable. I know. I've been there. It takes courage. One of my favorite quotes says, "Have the courage to make the change, the strength to get through it, and faith that everything will work out for the best." Embrace the courage to confront, to discover and to transform.

The results on the other side of this courage are tremendous. Your family will enjoy transformational conversations, collaborative intelligence, and a lasting legacy. Here are just a few of the benefits.

Conversation

You'll have purposeful conversations that break down current walls between one another. These conversations will allow you to see possibilities in yourself, in your family members, and in your family enterprise. You'll have an incredible sense of alignment, oneness, and trust as you pursue possibility together.

Intelligence

You'll nurture collaborative intelligence, where you all work and think together. You'll be able to see your differences as a strength, as you cultivate your intellectual diversity. You are better able to solve enterprise challenges as you discover solutions together, increasing productivity, creativity, and innovation.

Legacy

You'll enjoy a legacy of transformation and leave a transformational legacy. Through discovery of ideas, you'll be able to adapt and transform your enterprise to be relevant, becoming future-proofed. Through future-proofing and continued longevity, your family enterprise continues to generate employment, be a helm in communities, and precipitate social change.

To move from lifetime to legacy, it's important for your family to focus on the 3Cs:

- Clarity: Gaining clarity of shared vision, shared mission, and shared values as a family
- Communication: Communicating not just on the technical elements of the family enterprise, but also on the emotional elements

- Collaboration: Moving from individual rulership to collaborative leadership as a family, where we co-create the future of the enterprise.

This is all done through a platform of conversation.

To get started, you can plan a family meeting where you begin to practice collaborative leadership. I've put together a Quick Start Guide to help you in this process, which you may find useful. You can find it in a free downloadable workbook available on www.nikeanani.com/workbook. In it you will also find a Cheat Guide with a list of ten topics to have a conversation about in your first family meeting, in addition to practical exercises you can do together to help build connectivity.

The road from lifetime to legacy can be lonely. It's important to get in community with people towing a similar journey for learning, support, and inspiration. It's also important to continue reading. In the workbook, I have included information on communities to consider exploring and joining. I've also included further reading that would be useful.

For more information on me you may visit my website on www.nikeanani.com where you can find additional resources to support you in your journey toward legacy, including my podcast, The Connected Generation. On the podcast, I share best practices in building legacy enterprises; I also interview family business owners and thought leaders in the space.

To stay in touch, you may join my mailing list on my website or email me at na@nikeanani.com.

About Nike Anani

Nike Anani is an entrepreneur and a consultant. She was rated as a top-100 Family Business Consultant globally. She helps her clients bridge the gap between the senior and younger generations. As a result, they communicate, collaborate, and collectively gain clarity, to increase profit and productivity in their family businesses.

Nike works privately with select business families. Her clients choose to engage her not only because of her extensive professional training, but also because of her practical extensive experience (over a decade) as both a business founder and a next gen. This allows her to uniquely empathize with both generations and act as a connector.

Nike is passionate about diversity, and celebrates the uniqueness in every individual, family, and business. As such, her approach is highly customized for each client and not cookie-cutter.

You can find her as @nikeanani on LinkedIn, Twitter, Facebook, Instagram, and YouTube.

Connect With Me

I would love to hear about your journey. You may reach me directly at na@nikeanani.com or on my website www.nikeanani.com, where you will find additional resources to support you in your journey toward legacy, including my podcast, *The Connected Generation*. On the podcast, I share best practices in building legacy enterprises; I also interview family-business owners and thought leaders in the space.

References

1 "The Neuroscience of Trust," Paul J.Zak, *Harvard Business Review* (January – February 2017)

2 Wealth X, "Applied Wealth Intelligence," *Very High Net Worth Handbook 2021*

3 Dennis T. Jaffe and James Grubman, "Why the Second Generation Can Make or Break Your Family Business," *Harvard Business Review*

4 Dennis T. Jaffe, *Resilience of 100-Year Family Enterprises: How Opportunistic Innovation, Business Discipline, and a Culture of Stewardship Guide the Journey Across Generations*

5 James Clear, *Atomic Habits*

6 Simon Sinek, *Leaders Eat Last*

7 Juliet Bourke, *Which Two Heads Are Better Than One? How Diverse Teams Create Breakthrough Ideas and Make Smarter Decisions*, Australian Institute of Company Directors, 2016

8 Juliet Bourke, "The diversity and inclusion revolution: Eight powerful truths." *Deloitte Review*, issue 22

9 Sonnenfeld, Jeffrey, *The Hero's Farewell*

10 Tom Lahti, Marja-Liisa Halko, Necmi Karagozoglu and Joakim Wincent, "Why and how do founding entrepreneurs bond with their ventures? Neural correlates of entrepreneurial and parental bonding." *Journal of Business Venturing,* Volume 34, Issue 2, March 2019.

11 Jeff Greenberg, Sheldon Solomon, Tom Pyszczynski, "Terror Management Theory of Self-Esteem and Cultural Worldviews: Empirical Assessments and Conceptual Refinements," *Advances in Experimental Social Psychology*, Volume 29, 1997, Pages 61–139

12 T.H. Homes and R.H. Rahe, "The Social Readjustment Rating Scale." *Journal of Psychosomatic Research*, 196

13 RBC/Campden Wealth Limited, "The Next Generation of Global Enterprising Families: Shaping Tomorrow, Today," 2020

14 Eric J. Schoenberg, "When too much is not enough: Inherited wealth and the psychological meaning of money."

15 James E. Hughes Jr., Esq., Joanie Bronfman Ph.D., Jacqueline Merrill, M.B.A., "Reflections on Fiscal Unequals."

16 RBC / Campden Wealth, "The Next Generation of Global Enterprising Families: Shaping Tomorrow, Today," 202

17 PWC's Global Next gen Survey 2019

18 PWC's Global Next gen Survey 2019

19 Erik Erikson Stages of Psychosocial Development

20 Pew Research Center, "The Whys and Hows of Generations Research"

21 Amy Westervelt, *Forget "Having It All": How America Messed Up Motherhood--and How to Fix It*

22 Kelin E. Gersick et al, *Generation to Generation: Life Cycles of the Family Business*

23 Kelin E. Gersick et al, *Generation to Generation: Life Cycles of the Family Business*

24 Clive Seale, "Cancer Heroics: A Study of News Reports with Particular Reference to Gender," *British Sociological Association*

25 Sajuyigbe, Oyedele and Unachukwu, "Succession Planning and Generational Transition: The Greatest Challenges for Family-Owned Businesses in Nigeria"

26 Dennis T. Jaffe PhD and James Grubman PhD, *Cross Cultures: How Global Families Negotiate Change Across Generations*

27 Chris Cancialosi, "4 Reasons Social Capital Trumps All," *Forbes,* Sep 22, 2014

28 Basem Abbas Al Ubaidi, "Cost of Growing up in Dysfunctional Family," *Journal of Family Medicine and Disease Prevention*, July 31, 2017

29 T. C. Bergstrom, "On the economics of polygyny"; J. Hartung, "Polygyny and inheritance of wealth," *Current Anthropology*

30 Paul Vallely, "The Big Question: What's the history of polygamy, and how serious a problem is it in Africa?", *Independent*

31 Salman Elbedour et. al., "The Effect of Polygamous Marital Structure on Behavioural, Emotional, and Academic Adjustment in Children: A Comprehensive Review of the Literature," *Clinical Child and Family Psychology Review*, December 2002

32 P.N. Gwanfogbe et. al., "Polygyny and Marital Life Satisfaction: An Exploratory Study from Rural Cameroon," *Journal of Comparative Family Studies*, 1970

33 Martha Henriques, "Can the legacy of trauma be passed down the generations?", BBC

34 Ogbujah Columbus, "African Cultural Values and Inter-communal Relations: The Case with Nigeria," *Developing Country Studies*, 2021

35 2018 Ibrahim Index of African Governance

36 CIA, "Nigeria," *The World Factbook*

37 Marjorie Keniston McIntosh, *Yoruba Women, Work, and Social Changes*, 2009

38 Toyin Falola, "Yoruba Caravan System of the Nineteenth Century," *The International Journal of African Historical Studies*, 1991

39 DeCiantis and Lansberg, "Resilience in Family Enterprises," 2017

40 Chinua Achebe, *Things Fall Apart*

41 On Amir, "Tough Decisions: How Making Decisions Tires Your Brain," *Scientific America*

42 Elena Lytkina Botelho, Kim Rosenkoetter Powell, Stephen Kincaid, and Dina Wang, "What Sets Successful CEOs Apart," *Harvard Business Review*, 2017

43 Research conducted by Professor Steve Miller

44 Sajuyigbe, Oyedele and Unachukwu, *Succession Planning and Generational Transition: The Greatest Challenges for Family-Owned Businesses in Nigeria*

45 Rebecca A Meyer, *Accidental Partnerships: A new lens on sibling and cousin partnerships*

46 Ben Revill, "Millennials and their Money: Predictions for the Great Wealth Transfer," *Finance Digest*

47 Susan Sorenson, "How Employee Engagement Drives Growth," *Gallup Workplace*

48 Family Business Institute, *Family Business In Transition: Data and Analysis*, 2016

49 Roy Williams and Vic Preisser, *Preparing Heirs: Five Steps to a Successful Transition of Family Wealth and Values*

50 Quentin J. Fleming, *Keep the Family Baggage Out of the Family Business: Avoiding the Seven Deadly Sins That Destroy Family Businesses*

51 John Ward, *Perpetuating the Family Business*

52 Lyn Christian, "Conversational Intelligence®: A Path to Effective Leadership," SoulSalt

53 Lyn Christian, "Conversational Intelligence®: A Path to Effective Leadership," SoulSalt

54 David. R. Novak, "Killing the Myth that 93% of Conversation is Nonverbal," *What You Think You Know about Communication is Wrong*, March 17, 2020

55 Dr. Amy Edmondson, *The Fearless Organization: Creating Psychological Safety in the Workplace for Learning, Innovation, and Growth*

56 Amy Edmondson, "Psychological Safety and Learning Behaviour in Work Teams," *Administrative Science Quarterly*, 1999

57 Juliet Bourke, "The diversity and inclusion revolution: Eight powerful truths," *Deloitte Review*, issue 22

58 Juliet Bourke, "The diversity and inclusion revolution: Eight powerful truths," *Deloitte Review*, issue 22

59 Dr Timothy Clark, *The 4 Stages of Psychological Safety: Defining the Path to Inclusion and Innovation*

60 Michel Marie Deza and Elena Deza, "Distances in Applied Social Sciences," *Encyclopedia of Distances*, 2014

CPSIA information can be obtained
at www.ICGtesting.com
Printed in the USA
LVHW040107010722
722529LV00011B/942

9 781922 357366